Management Information Systems and Statistics

Frances and **Roland Bee** work as personnel and training consultants in their own business, Time *for* People Ltd, which they set up in 1985. They have a wide range of public- and private-sector clients, including some in retail, transportation, electronics, the universities and local government.

Frances read mathematics at Oxford and statistics at London University. Her early career was in research and strategic planning at the GLC. On completion of her MBA at the Management College, Henley, she transferred to the personnel and training field. She moved into senior management with Abbey National and then into retail with the John Lewis Partnership, occupying several senior posts such as assistant finance director and general manager of a large department store.

Roland started as a chemist with Fisons Fertilisers before serving in the RAF as a navigator. Following this he worked at a senior level in personnel and management services roles in local authorities, including seven years as a chief officer. During this time he obtained his MA from Henley. Subsequently he worked for the London Electricity Board (as chief O&M officer) and the Housing Corporation (as personnel services manager).

They are co-authors of two other IPD publications: *Training Needs Analysis and Evaluation* (1994); and *Customer Care* (1995), part of the Training Extras series. Another Training Extras title, on *Constructive Feedback*, will be published in 1996.

The Institute of Personnel and Development is the leading publisher of books and reports for personnel and training professionals and students and for all those concerned with the effective management and development of people at work. For full details of all our titles please telephone the Publishing Department on 0181 263 3387.

Management Studies Series

Series Editors: Michael Armstrong and David Farnham

The IPD examination system provides a unique route into professional personnel practice. The Management Studies Series forms the essential reading for all IPD personnel students.

Case Studies in Personnel
ed. Diana Winstanley and Jean Woodall

Tutors' Manual
ed. Diana Winstanley and Jean Woodall

Passing Your IPM Exams
Elaine Crosthwaite

Management Studies 1

Finance and Accounting for Managers
Second Edition
David Davies

The Corporate Environment
Second Edition
David Farnham

Management Information Systems and Statistics
Roland and Frances Bee

Management Processes and Functions
Michael Armstrong

Managing Human Resources
Second Edition
Jane Weightman

Management Studies 2

Employee Development
Rosemary Harrison

Employee Relations
David Farnham

Employee Resourcing
*Derek Torrington, Laura Hall,
Isabel Haylor and Judith Myers*

MANAGEMENT STUDIES 1

Management Information Systems and Statistics

Roland and Frances Bee

Institute of Personnel and Development

To our daughter Elizabeth Alice Bee
5 April 1988

First published in 1990
Reprinted 1990, 1993, 1995

Phototypeset by Wessex Typesetters, Frome, Somerset
and printed in Great Britain by Short Run Press, Exeter.

British Library Cataloguing-in-Publication Data

A catalogue record for this book is available from the British Library

ISBN 0–85292–435–6

The views expressed in this book are the authors' own and
may not necessarily reflect those of the IPD.

**INSTITUTE OF PERSONNEL
AND DEVELOPMENT**

IPD House, Camp Road, London SW19 4UX
Tel: 0181 971 9000   Fax: 0181 263 3333
Registered office as above. Registered Charity No. 1038333
A company limited by guarantee. Registered in England No. 2931892

Contents

List of Figures

List of Tables

Editors' Foreword

Today's business environment demands that managers possess a wide range of knowledge, skills and competencies. As well as a sound understanding of management processes and functions, managers need to be able to make the best use of their time and talents, and of other people's, and to work with and through others to achieve corporate objectives. They also need to demonstrate a full understanding of the business environment and of their organization's key resources: its people, finance and information.

Management education in Britain has at last begun to take full account of these business realities. In particular, the Professional Management Foundation Programme is a major initiative developed by a group of forward-looking professional institutes to meet these needs. They recognize that a synthesis of knowledge and skills, and theory and practice, is vital for all managers and those aspiring to management positions.

For many years, the Institute of Personnel Management has been strongly committed to developing professional excellence. This major new series reflects this ideal. It covers five key areas: management processes and functions; the corporate environment; managing human resources; management information systems and statistics; and finance and accounting for managers. In drawing on the expertise of experienced teachers and managers, this series provides all students of management with an invaluable set of practical, introductory and informed texts on contemporary management studies.

Michael Armstrong
David Farnham
April 1990

Introduction

We are living in a time of great change – characterized by an increasingly professional approach to management. No longer are good managers considered to be born, but instead hatched out after a gestation period of management education and training. Perhaps it would be fair to say that management is more and more viewed as a science rather than an art. No longer is it acceptable, if indeed it ever was, to base our decisions on hunch, intuition, or *back of a cigarette packet*, approaches. This is not to say that experience and judgement are not vital attributes, but in the fast moving world of business today the successful manager will need to have a portfolio of quantitative techniques to deploy in his/her decision making processes.

The developments in management thinking have led to developments in management education. A number of professional institutes have combined to form the Consultative Council of Professional Management Organizations (CCPMO) which has been discussing a common approach to management education. From this, the Institute of Chartered Secretaries and Administrators, the Institute of Administrative Management, the Institute of Personnel and Development and the Institute of Purchasing and Supply have joined to provide the Professional Management Foundation Programme. This book is the definitive text for the subjects of management information systems, statistics and information technology in the core syllabus of the common first year. It is not simply an introduction to these subjects but an introductory book for managers who wish to gain a greater understanding of the figures relating to their organizations. We believe it will also provide a useful starting point for all those taking their first steps in the world of converting data to information.

Drawing on examples from across the business world, we address some of the quantitative aspects of management. Our approach is to assume that you know little about the subjects, other than being able to cope with the basic mathematical functions, and to take you gently through to a reasonable level of understanding. We will not try and convert you into professional Statisticians, but we hope to share with you an awareness of the value of the *numbers* in this world of business and organization management. We are aiming to give you sufficient understanding of some of the most useful statistical techniques to recognize when they might be helpful in your business or professional activities. Some are straightforward enough for any manager to apply themselves, others may require the help of a friendly neighbourhood (or in your case, Company) Statistician.

The techniques are only a means to an end – they are not an end in themselves. They are a means of taking the manager from the chaos of the Dark Ages of the data through to the renaissance of information. Data on its own is meaningless, it must be converted into information before it can be used in the decision making process. We suggest that you think of the techniques as an engine converting raw fuel into usable energy and then into power. As all you managers know, information is power and that is what statistics, properly applied, can give you.

Statisticians are a breed unto themselves. They talk fluent Martian – or so it sounds to the layman. Why do they have such fixations on 'x's and 'y's? Why do they have the need to revert to a language and alphabet more familiar to Plato than to a Captain of Industry? Being a Statistician appears to go hand in hand with an inability or an unwillingness to communicate with their less numerate brothers and sisters.

We, on the other hand, are not going to blind you with jargon. We shall try and explain the terms as we go along, using capital letters for emphasis when we introduce a term in its relevant section for the first time, then provide the definition in the Glossary of Terms at the end of the book. We hope that by the time you encounter them you will be able to take them in your stride. We promise that we take you gently by the hand – there is nothing to fear, in fact we hope that you will find it at least interesting and challenging. Above all, we hope to demonstrate that it can help you in your business and your profession.

Now, a word about the layout of this book. Part 1 starts out with an introduction to management information systems. It goes on to examine management information in the context of the organization – its structures and cultures. Finally, in Part 1 we discuss some of the issues that are considered important in the design and implementation of management information systems. Part 2 deals with statistics – numbers into information. Hopefully, we are able to break through some of the mystique of this subject and we try to present it in a way that the non-numerate arts graduate or someone at about GCE 'A' level, moving into business and management, will take to the subject. We proceed in a fairly gentle fashion with plenty of examples, increasing the tempo a little as we move into some of the more powerful but surprisingly practical techniques. Part 3 then takes a look at information technology – starting from scratch with a look at what is a computer. We move on to look at information applications on the computer and finish with operational applications where the computer controls the process.

There may be occasions when, for the sake of simplicity in our explanations, we will offend the pure Statistician/Mathematician. We make no apology for this. We have already stated our view that statistics for most managers are the means to, not the end of, understanding the business process. When you get to the final line where the professional Statistician has calculated 'x' equal to something and therefore served his or her purpose, you the aspiring business manager will continue to use this computed or calculated value of 'x' to make your inferences about what is happening in the business. The core philosophy of our approach is that management information systems, statistics and information technology are not theoretical subjects, ends in themselves, but the means to a greater understanding of the business process.

Finally, our thanks go to John Bevan of the University of Kent for his help and advice on the statistical sections and to John McFarlane for his helpful comments on the information technology sections.

ROLAND and FRANCES BEE
Tewin Wood

Part 1

Management Information Systems

'What You Need to Know'

'Management Information Systems' may sound grand, yet the term refers to a very basic but vital concept. Management information is the life blood of any business or organization. It can range from simple reports on sales and profits for a small company through to complex systems covering all aspects of a vast conglomerate. Management information is in essence what you, the Manager, need to know to run your business successfully. The system is merely the mechanism to ensure that information is available to you in the form you want it and when you need it.

Chapter 1 introduces you to management information systems. Chapter 2 looks at management information systems in the context of different types of organization. Finally, Chapter 3 covers the important issues that need to be considered when designing and implementing a management information system.

1

Introduction

What is Management Information?

Management information has become something of an in-phrase. The popularity of management information is not surprising nor illfounded as it is a vital ingredient in the superior performance of every successful organization. What we sometimes forget is that management information is not new – it has been around for a very long time. Perhaps what is new and different is the realization that the value of management information is critically dependent on three main factors:

a   the content of the information;
b   the form in which it is presented;
c   the timing of its presentation.

For our purposes we choose to define MANAGEMENT INFORMATION as:

> the right information in the right form at the right time, so enabling the manager effectively and efficiently to do his/her job.

The starting point for understanding what management information is required is the realization that it is dependent on who requires it and for what purpose. Throughout any organization there will be managers with specific jobs and responsibilities – each with their own particular management information needs which might change from time to time. In an ideal world a Management Information System (MIS) would be tailored to the needs of the individual manager but in today's world this is not always possible. Managers may have to make do with data which

3

is produced for other purposes and convert it as best they can to meet their own requirements. However, the developments in computer technology are increasingly making it possible for managers to select the information they require, in the form best suited to their needs and when they want it. More about this later!

Management Functions

Before we go on any further to talk about management information, let us digress slightly for a moment, to look at the functions of management, that is, what managers actually do. For convenience of explanation they are often defined under three main headings:

a   strategic planning/planning;
b   organizing/implementing;
c   controlling/reviewing.

However, contained within each of these main headings is a multiplicity of different tasks which, depending on the structure and culture of the organization, are performed at a variety of different levels. On the planning side the tasks can range from the strategic level of setting objectives and policy formulation for the organization as a whole, down to the operational level of planning a specific task. Similarly, this range is mirrored for the functions of organizing and control. However, the boundaries between these functions are not clear cut but are often hazy. There are frequent overlaps between them and they are not always sequential. Perhaps the functions can be better set out not as a list but as some sort of cyclic process with *information flows* to and fro around the cycle, as shown in Figure 1.1.

Of necessity, this is an over-simplified model depicting the management processes. The important points for us to remember are that there are different functions and levels of management and that the process is cyclic in nature. In order for us to proceed through this cycle, information is required at each stage. We shall now look at the different functions and the types of information that might be required to perform them.

Figure 1.1
The Management Function Cycle

Strategic Planning

We define strategic planning as the setting of overall objectives and policies for an organization. In order to do this the organization will need to scan its environment by examining such issues as:

What are the current objectives, and how well have they been achieved in the past?	– measured by sales, sales growth, profit, profit growth, etc.
Where is the organization in the market place?	– measured by market share.

What are its strengths and weaknesses? — these can be seen in terms of its resources – people, finance, physical, etc.

(human resource audit) — in people terms, such factors as the skills and expertise of the workforce are an important ingredient on the credit side, while skill shortages and employee relations problems will show on the debit side.

(financial appraisal) — in financial terms, it can be the strength of the balance sheet, current profitability, cash flow, etc.

(physical resource audit) — in physical terms, such resources as buildings, plant equipment, technology, location, etc., are important.

What is the organization's standing at the moment, that is, does the business community regard the organization as being well run with an optimum use of resources? Is it in a SUNRISE or SUNSET industry? — indicated by share value, media comment, city broker bulletins, etc.

What is happening in the environment in which the organization functions, for example, to market trends, population trends, attitudes, economic trends, social trends, legal changes, political changes? — use of market research surveys to investigate attitudes and demand, awareness of legal and political activity, etc.

Planning

The next stage involves the detailed planning to turn the overall objectives and policies into targets. These can be, for example, production targets, sales targets or financial targets. Then, for each particular target a plan will be derived to achieve that target and that plan which will depend on the resources that are available:

Physical, in terms of land, buildings, plant, etc.	– measured by floor space, machine capacity, etc.
Human, in terms of employees.	– measured in terms of numbers and skills, etc.
Financial.	– measured in terms of cash flow, capital, revenue, etc.

At this stage, both for the target setting and the planning process, timescale will be all important. Sales targets may be expressed in terms of sales volumes per month or year, production targets may be set in terms of units per quarter or per half-year and the objective will be to achieve these targets within the given timescales.

Organizing/Implementing

Organizing and implementing involves the day-to-day management of the plan, working out detailed schedules of work, allocating people to tasks, motivating and leading them, handling the immediate finances of the organization. The actual information needs will, of course, vary according to the nature of the work. Examples could be information on daily production by machine/person, machine running time, material wastage, incidence of equipment breakdown, staff absence rates, productivity rates, etc. The point that we would make is that probably all the information needed to organize the work or to implement the plan is available somewhere in the *system*. The problem is that it is usually hidden as DATA and the principal purpose of this book is to help you through the process of converting the data into management information.

Controlling and Reviewing

Controlling and reviewing involves managers in *measuring the performance* – of individuals and sections against their targets, and of the whole organization against its strategic objectives. Are targets being achieved on time? Are the costs of achieving the targets within budget? If not, how far out are they? How close to target do they need to be, what is the acceptable range of performance? In the light of what is achieved we may need to revise our targets, plans, policies and even our overall objectives, and the cycle begins again. In order to be able to answer these questions and complete our management cycle we need appropriate management information, in a form we can use and at a time when we can take the necessary corrective action to achieve our objectives.

Hopefully this very brief summary of the management process has helped indicate both the variety of purposes for which management information is required and the enormous range of different types of information involved. You will recall that at the beginning of this chapter we stated that the value or quality of management information depended on three factors:

a   the content of the information;
b   the form or presentation of the information;
c   the timing of its presentation.

We have already begun to look at the question of *what information* is required and to show that the use or purpose to which that information is to be put is the key factor in deciding what information to produce. We are now going to look at the next factor – the form, or presentation, of management information.

Presentation of Information

If we know what information we require, you may say to yourself, what more is there to consider? It is in the answer to that question, we believe, that the whole art of designing a management information system lies. Let us take a simple example of a company that manufactures glass bottles in 20 factories across the country. Consider the information needs of the Supervisor of a particular production line, and compare these with the information needs of the Managing Director of the company. The Supervisor will need detailed information on the production line for which s/he is responsible. The Managing Director (MD) will be more concerned with total production for the whole company and will probably not need to have information broken down to less than factory level. It is highly unlikely (unless there is a specific reason, such as an experimental production line) that the Managing Director will need information about an individual production line. So both managers will need information on production, but at quite different levels of detail. The MD's powers of understanding, analysis and decision making will be completely swamped by the sheer volume of information provided if it comes to him/her in the same degree of detail needed by the Supervisor. On the other hand the Supervisor would find that the lack of detail provided for the MD would be totally inappropriate for his/her needs.

So we can see that one important issue affecting the way in which management information should be presented is the level of detail needed. Also, we have seen that there can be as much danger in having too much information as in having too little. Indeed, with the use of computers in the routine operation of business processes we have the ability to produce masses and masses of information and the problem often becomes one of too much information rather than not enough. It is easier to churn it all out than to think how it should be modified to meet the needs of individual managers. Ackoff, as long ago as 1967, in a classic article 'Management Misinformation Systems'[1] argued that most Management Information Systems (MIS's) were designed on the assumption that managers lacked the relevant information, whereas he believed that most managers suffered from an over-abundance of irrelevant information! Even casual observation of the offices and desks of managers today suggests that Ackoff's message has not been heard. In these days of the electronic office we still see evidence of the massive piles of computer printout that hit managers' desks from time to time. When we shift the emphasis from *supplying* relevant information to *eliminating* irrelevant information, then the two most important activities become *filtration* and *condensation* – we filter out the irrelevant and condense the relevant into manageable form.

The use of statistical techniques, which are described later in this book, is often the key to the successful conversion of data into information and to its presentation in a usable form. These techniques can be used to summarize data and present it in a form highlighting the significant points of interest, thereby making them more readily understood by the reader.

Let us look at another simple example. Suppose we are interested in the number of working days lost through employee absenteeism. The basic data would be in number of days lost, perhaps broken down by department. However, this can be pretty meaningless on its own. We can use statistical techniques to present information in a way which means something immediately to the reader, for example, by presenting the absentee figures as a proportion of days lost compared with working man-days available. If these proportions were broken down by department we could compare the figures and take appropriate action. For example:

We have two departments, A and B. A has 200 days lost through absence during the year while department B has only 75 days lost. Which department has the better absence figures?

At first sight we might be tempted to say that department B has the better figure because, as everyone knows, 75 is less than 200.

However, the statistician would compare the absences with the possible working days available. Let us assume that department A had 20,000 working man-days while department B had 5,000 working man-days available. The comparison looks like this:

Department A
$$\frac{200}{20,000} = 0.01\ (1\%)$$

Department B
$$\frac{75}{5,000} = 0.015\ (1.5\%)$$

Department B, far from being better, is now shown to be half as bad again as Department A, so management would probably decide to concentrate attention on Department B. By presenting the absence figures in this way we actually produce information on which management can take action. In the above example, the absence *rates*, expressed as a proportion or percentage of days lost against employee availability, give a much more useful picture of the absence levels in the two departments than the raw absence *figures*.

Often an item of information is meaningless on its own. For example, suppose we are interested in the productivity of a sales representative measured in terms of sales/year. Let us imagine Mr X achieves sales of £100,000 per year. Is this a good, bad or indifferent performance? We just do not know. How can we possibly tell? Well, we could compare his results with the other sales representatives. However, if there are 100 sales persons, it could be a bit difficult to compare 100 sales/year figures and make much sense out of it all. So what do we do? Perhaps we could:

a list the results of all the sales people in order from the highest results at the top down to the lowest sales/year at the bottom and see where Mr X's result falls;

b compare his performance with the average performance of all sales representatives;

c as a complete alternative, compare his performance over time. What sales results did he achieve last year, or over the last five years?

You may now be beginning to realize that management information is a complex subject. However, as we have seen, the basic principles are fairly simple and so long as we keep these in our mind we will be neither overwhelmed nor disappointed in our pursuit of management information. So far we have looked at *what information* and *how should it be presented*. We look next at the third key issue – *when is it required?*

Timeliness of Information

This is often an issue that can be overlooked in the quest for the right information in the right form but, no matter how good the information or how well it is presented, if it arrives too late it is useless. A good example of the timeliness of information is the difference between financial accounting and management accounting, described in detail in the companion book in this series.[2] The distinction between them is that financial accounting gives an accurate *historical record* of the results of the year's trading activities, while management accounting gives an *up-to-date comparison* of how the business is performing against budgeted targets. Management accounting gives the information to managers in time for them to take corrective action to secure the results they are aiming for.

The frequency with which the information is presented to management is also very important. If it is arriving too frequently it can over-load the manager. If the intervals between its arrival are too long then it is possible that it will be arriving too late for its purpose. For example, if we are concerned about meeting a weekly target, say the sales of a particular product, then we will probably want information on a daily basis. We will also want the latest information, for example, yesterday's sales figures on our desk when we get into work this morning. If it is yearly sales that are particularly important then monthly reports will probably be sufficient and the timing of their arrival will not be critical, at least at the beginning of the yearly cycle. However, this is a particularly good example for considering the timeliness of information in that, as the year progresses, the arrival of the *latest figures* will be eagerly awaited and in the final two months the interval of reporting may well be reduced to weekly. This change in interval is because there is decreasing time left for the manager to make corrections to ensure that targets are met.

Well, we have looked at what information, in what form and when it is required. Now we look at how managers receive their information – the different types, or classes, of report that are generally used.

Classes of Management Information Reports

There are usually considered to be four main classes of reports through which information may be made available to management. They are:

a   routine reports;
b   exception reports;
c   request reports;
d   special reports.

As the name suggests, ROUTINE REPORTS are the regular reports that are the bedrock of any manager's information system. They are characterized by the fact that they will usually arrive at regular, pre-determined time intervals and contain the same type of information presented in exactly the same format on each occasion.

Examples would be weekly sales reports, monthly reports on absenteeism, half-yearly reports on staff turnover, annual reports to staff and shareholders, etc.

The second class of report, the EXCEPTION REPORT, is generated as the result of some exceptional situation. For example, it could be that as Production Manager we are interested in the performance of each production line. But are we? In fact, we may only be interested in receiving reports from those production lines that, *by exception*, do not achieve their targets. By asking only for these exception reports we would cut down on the amount of information we have to study, allowing us to concentrate our attention on those parts of the operation which have not been going according to plan. Another example could be where we are managing a shop or a store with a vast number of products. We are clearly interested to know from time to time exactly how many items we have in each stock line, but we would want to know immediately the details of any item that goes out of stock. Hence we would probably want, *by exception*, daily reports only on out-of-stock items. If we are conscious of the costs of over-stocking we would probably want exceptional, weekly reports on those item lines which exceed particular target limits. Alternatively, we might be the Personnel Manager responsible for a number of factories or premises. Suppose absenteeism is a concern. We would probably be inundated with information if we received reports from all factories. So we would seek exception reports only from those factories where the absentee rate is greater than a particular level, say, 5%. What we have decided is that we are not worried about those premises with absentee rates below 5%; they require no action to be taken by us at the present time. However, we are worried about all those premises with absentee rates over 5% and we will wish to take action on them or at least be sure that action is being taken.

Exception reports are really a more sophisticated version of routine reports. They have the advantage that they focus on the *problem* areas, the areas where action or decisions may be required.

REQUEST REPORTS are those produced as a result of a specific request for information thought to be available but not usually included in the routine report. They may provide information in more detail, for example, staff turnover shown by the factories in the group rather than as an overall figure. They may provide information required for a specific timescale, for example, we may be interested in one month's figures on profitability rather than waiting for the half-yearly report. A request report could be a report that other managers receive as a routine report but we do not. As the Finance Manager, for example, we might not routinely receive information on market trends which the Marketing Manager would – but we would find such information invaluable at certain times, perhaps when we are putting together the budget for next year.

Of course, the computer has the flexibility to produce request reports more easily then we were able to do in the days before substantial computer power was generally available. In parallel with the developments in computing there is a growing school of thought that most reports should be request reports and that routine reports should be kept to the minimum. The advances in computer technology, with the prospect of most managers having immediate access to a computer or computer terminal, is making this more and more likely. Moves in this direction will be accompanied by a shift away from what might be thought as the more traditional management information systems to a relatively new concept often referred to as corporate database systems. However, more of this later.

Finally, we come to the SPECIAL REPORT. As the name implies, the need for this type of report usually arises out of some *special* or unusual situation and may require information which is not readily available and which may require some special exercise in data capture. By their very nature, the need for special reports should arise infrequently, at least in those organizations which have sorted out their information requirements. They will usually have to be designed from scratch specifically for the particular requirement and often will be very expensive to produce. A typical example could be when a factory puts out a particularly poor production result one month. There could be a call for a lot of detailed information on that factory, for example, details of employees, the plant and equipment, specific production line figures, etc. Another example could be where an opportunity has arisen to sell our product for the first time in a foreign country, perhaps we have been approached by an agent from that country. We will want information about that country, for example, details of its markets, its economy and its import regulations. That information will almost certainly not be available within our organization and considerable external research will be required.

In this section we have looked at the types or classes of reports through which management information is made available. We will be beginning to get a feel for both the potential of management information and the sort of choices that have to be made in designing our Management Information System. However, one very important issue which cannot be overlooked when designing our MIS is the cost of getting the right information in the right form at the right time and we look at this briefly in the next section.

Cost of Management Information

Having management information is generally considered to be a good thing, although we have already seen that too much can be both wasteful and counter-productive. However, even the production of really useful management information may be considered too costly and we need always to bear in mind the benefits of having the information weighed up against the cost of producing it.

Let us look at some of the typical costs involved:

a the costs of collecting and recording the basic data;
b the cost of processing the information;
c the costs of printing, duplicating and distributing the reports;
d the cost of the time taken to read, understand and digest the information by managers.

The costs of collecting and recording data vary widely, depending on the amount of data involved and the difficulties in obtaining it. For example, it is probably a lot easier to obtain data on the age of our employees (which is usually required for other purposes such as pension schemes) than on, perhaps, their qualifications. Similarly, total sales figures might be readily available but not broken down by type of product.

The costs of processing the information will depend on whether it is a manual or a computerized system. In the case of manual systems, it can take many manhours to convert the raw data into the management information required. In computerized systems, the costs arise rather differently and will include:

a   the cost of buying the equipment and setting up the system, for example, writing/adapting computer programs;
b   the cost of getting the data into the computer;
c   the cost of running the computer.

With regard to the cost incurred in printing and duplicating the reports, the sheer volume of paper in any large organization can be enormous and the logistics of getting the report to the right manager quickly can be an expensive headache. So are there any alternatives? Luckily for managers today there are – the electronic handling and transmission of information by computers is one of the major developments going on at present. This will be discussed in Chapter 14.

So far as the cost in terms of the time taken by managers to read, understand and digest the information is concerned, some may say that surely this is an essential part of the manager's job. We would agree but, as we have already shown, by presenting the right information in the right form for a manager at the right time (possibly by reporting only on those deviations from the plan) it should be possible to reduce considerably the amount of time a manager needs to spend on absorbing the relevant information.

All these cost factors emphasize the need to ensure that the information is really *required*, that it is being presented in the most appropriate form for the manager's use and that it is going to the right people.

Conclusion

In this chapter we have discussed what managers do and how the information needs vary between different managers and change over time. We have emphasized the requirement for management information to be timely, in the right form and directly relevant to the manager's needs. The principles we have covered are equally relevant to manual and to computer based information systems. We have looked at the different types of report through which information can be made available to managers and finally we examined the costs of management information. We have concentrated in this chapter on the information needs of the individual managers but, by and large, most managers work as part of an organization. In the next chapter we shall consider how the structure and type of organization can influence the management information system.

References

1 ACKOFF R L. 'Management Misinformation Systems', *Management Science*, 14, No. 4 (December 1967).
2 DAVIES D B. *Finance and Accounting for Managers* (IPM, 1990).

2

Management Information and the Organization

Introduction

When an organization is a small, simple set-up the need for management information can be virtually non-existent. In a small firm with an owner/manager and a small number of staff, that manager will probably know in detail every aspect of the business and will probably keep his/her own records of useful information. The situation becomes trickier if within this one business there are two different types of activity. For example, suppose the manager runs a decorating business and also has a shop selling paint, wallpaper, etc. Add to this a further dimension, say, a redevelopment is planned of the premises where the business is located – and now the manager could start to think that things are getting a little out of hand. The manager might begin to feel the need for some formal system of management information in order to allow him/her to prioritize the use of time and to concentrate on the important indicators of business success.

This is a simple example, and we have used it to introduce the very important concept that *the need for management information increases with the complexity of the organization, the complexity of the tasks carried out, and the rate of change in the environment of the organization.* From this statement it can be readily understood why there is an increasing emphasis on management information today. We have seen the growth of large complex organizations like the Hanson Trust – vast conglomerates of many different, disparate businesses. We have also seen companies, which we normally associate with one particular activity, now engaging in a variety of others. Take, for example, Woolworth's. We all know that through their high street stores Woolworth's offer a range of goods from records to confectionery. Did we also know that under their new corporate name of Kingfisher they are very big in the do-it-yourself business (B&Q Stores) and in retailing pharmaceuticals through their chain of chemists shops (Super Drug)? Also, as a major owner of prime commercial sites in most of our towns and cities, property management is a very important and profitable part of their business. Finally, like most major organizations today, the management of their finances is almost a business activity on its own. By the nature of the retail trade there will be day-to-day ebbs and flows of money through the business. That money can run into millions of pounds and it is important that it is put to good use all the time. Hence there will be a part of the Kingfisher operation which is dedicated to this function and which will be involved in investing the surplus funds, possibly in the stock exchange. In other words, Kingfisher is a conglomerate of many diverse activities. In fact, most large organizations today are a complex mix of different activities.

Another important factor is that we are now in a period of great change. Let's look at some of these changes:

- technological, for example, computers, robot production lines, etc.

- demographic, an aging population in the UK, smaller families, more sophisticated requirements and expectations from the consumer.

- international, the breakdown of national barriers, for example, the emergence of international companies or companies with worldwide interests. Perhaps the best examples of this type of change are the *single market* concept in the European Community which is effective from 1992, and the breaking down of political barriers in Eastern and Western Europe.

- social values, for example a greater concern for protecting the environment.

So, we have seen that not only are organizations becoming more complex and their activities more varied, but also that this is against a background of enormous changes in their environment. Hence there has come a burgeoning need for information and more emphasis on the development of management information systems. So what influences the type of management information system required? In part it will be the type of business the organization is operating, for example, manufacturing, services, etc., but equally important will be the management structure and what is known as the management *culture*. By structure of an organization we mean the way it is set out in departments, etc. Stonich explains[1] that culture

> can be identified as the way an organization performs a given set of tasks. It is the set of traditional and habitual ways of thinking, feeling and reacting to opportunities and problems that confront an organization. It is rooted in the past successes and failures of the organization.

Both structure and culture will influence the way management information flows through the organization so let's have a look at some of the differences in these two dimensions, and examine how they affect the need for and type of MIS.

Management Structures

There appears to be a general measure of agreement among management writers about the way in which management structures develop as an enterprise grows. Many organizations start with an owner/entrepreneur and a limited number of employees. There is usually a single product line at the beginning and a single channel for the distribution of this product. The owner/managers have personal control over both strategic and operating decisions and their information needs reflect the very direct nature of their interaction with their suppliers, the business itself, their customers and their environment. The management structure, with its information flows, is shown in Figure 2.1.

As the business grows there is a tendency to modify the structure by delegating specific parts or functions of the business to specialists, for example, production, sales/marketing, personnel, accounts/finance and research and development. There may well still be a single product line, possibly with some variations, and still a single channel or set of channels for distribution. Increasingly, performance assessment by the owner starts to become more objective than previously, against more sophisticated technical and cost criteria. By now the information needs may well be starting

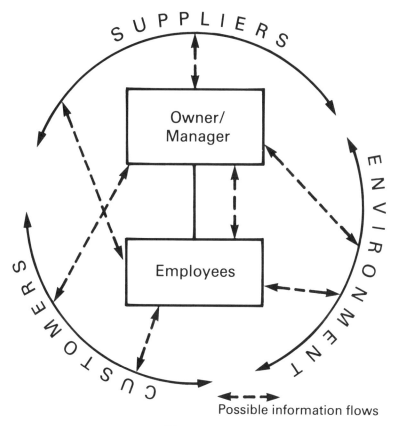

Figure 2.1
Simple Owner/Manager Structure

to become fairly complex. The owner/managers will need information on their suppliers and their raw materials, they will need information on competitors and marketing information such as market share, and they will need information on changes in the environment that will affect their markets in terms of threats and opportunities. When we recognize that environmental changes could cover such aspects as legal, economic, social and political issues; that information on supplies and suppliers will cover matters like changes in technology, costs, etc.; and that information on competitors and markets could be endless; we appreciate the need

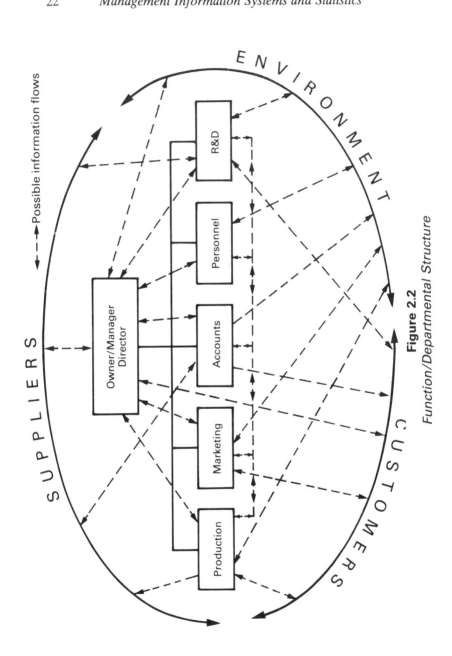

Figure 2.2
Function/Departmental Structure

to be selective, cost-conscious and very thoughtful about the design of our management information systems if they are to work to our advantage. The management structure at this stage of development, with its information flows, is shown in Figure 2.2.

Finally, as the business develops still further and diversifies into multiple product lines or multiple markets, the management structure may well develop to one where there is a division, or delegation of particular products or markets to other managers. To attempt to draw a map of the possible information flows on top of the formal management structures at this stage is about as complicated as drawing a diagram of a printed circuit board. The

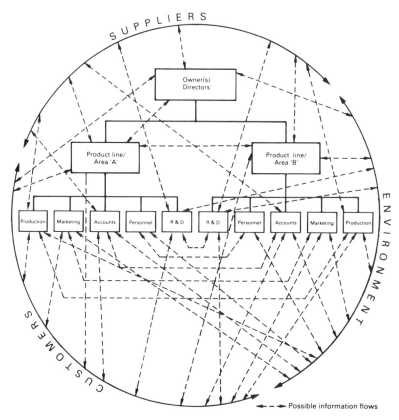

Figure 2.3
Complex Product/Division Structure

management structure and the information flows are shown in Figure 2.3. Notice how complicated the information flows become as the organization structure develops.

There is, of course, a wide variety of management structures that are different from the traditional ones discussed above. Some organizations might have no formal, recognized management structure at all. Others might be very complicated, allowing more than one reporting line from the operational manager to his/her managers – perhaps reporting on the one hand to a *senior professional manager* and on the other hand to another manager, a *project manager*, to whom s/he is on loan for a specific project. These two extremes of *no structure/very complex matrix* are often more to do with the culture in the organization than its structure, so we will discuss them in more detail in the next section.

Management Cultures

Before we move on it is perhaps appropriate to mention that organizations with the same, or similar, management structures may well have very different management information needs if their management style or culture is different. There are many different views on management culture. Let's have a look at a few examples based loosely on Handy's theories[2] and see how the management information needs might differ:

a   *Person culture.* A person culture will exist in those organizations which have a minimal structure, where people combine from choice, for example, partnerships, co-operatives and communes. Nobody is always or completely in charge. Everybody is 'doing their own thing' – and they like it that way. Information is usually shared on a 'need to know' basis and there is little need for formal management information systems. This culture flourishes in small professional practices such as those of solicitors or architects, as long as they stay small. At the basic level the management information needs are minmal. As organizations grow, to stay successful, they need to adjust to one of the other cultures, adapting their management information needs as they develop. The person culture can be shown diagrammatically (Figure 2.4):

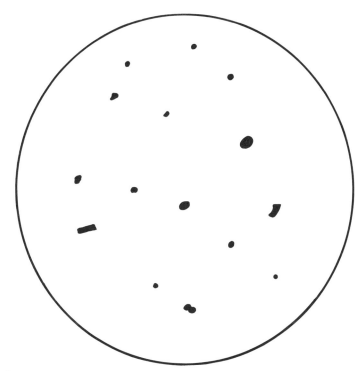

Size and shape of the dots represent differences in the individuals

Figure 2.4
Person Culture

b *Task culture.* A task culture often exists where the organization
is set up to manage specific tasks where the emphasis is on
getting the job done. It often operates under what is known as
a matrix or net structure where resources are regarded as being
under corporate rather than functional ownership and can be
called upon to be utilized under different managements from
time to time. It tends to operate where the business of
the organization is project orientated. There is little formal
structure outside of the project teams. It is very flexible and
reacts very well to different circumstances and copes very well
with constant and major changes. There is an emphasis on the
specialisms of team members. To operate this type of culture
successfully, the management information systems have to be

both corporate, helping to control business operations overall, and project orientated. Strategic business decisions are fed by the corporate information systems and the projects are managed by local information systems. Ideally, these local management information systems are capable of being integrated into the corporate information systems so that project performance reporting is made a by-product of the local reporting systems. A task culture can be shown diagrammatically as:

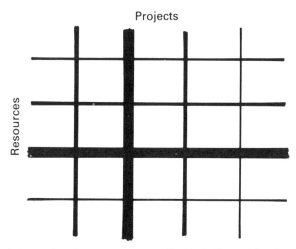

Size of the project/resources controlled is indicated by the thickness of the line

Figure 2.5
Task Culture

c   *Power culture.* Sometimes known as a web culture because of the similarity to a spider's web. Power is centralized in the hands of the owner/manager or the Board of Directors, etc. This culture is often found in entrepreneurial organizations which are dominated by an individual or group. This style works best where the organization is small. The route to growth for this culture is to have satellite organizations around the periphery. There are clear management information flows from the operational level to the satellites and from the satellites to the centre of the web, so that centralized management decisions can be made correctly. A particular need is that information gets to the centre very quickly and usually this can only be achieved in organizations of any size by the use of computers. It can be shown diagrammatically as:

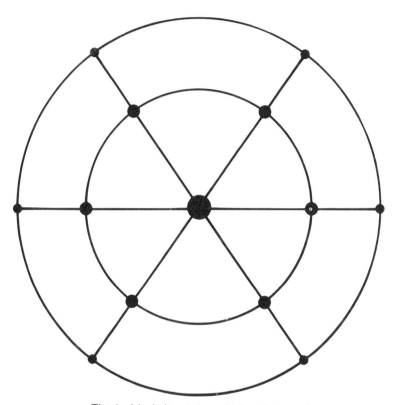

The 'spider' sits at the middle of the web

Figure 2.6
Power Culture

d   *Role culture.* Sometimes known as a temple culture, it is where the organization is clearly controlled from the top and is divided into the different functions, for example, finance, sales/marketing, production, etc. It has the benefit usually of being ordered, procedural and rational. This culture appears to be favoured by the bureaucracies. It is run by rules, possibly stifling initiative, but is fair to all concerned as everybody knows the rules and they are applied in the same way to all in the organization. In terms of information flows they tend to be structured and organized. They run up and down the functions, with instructions going from the Management Board to the operational level, and with results being reported back to the top management, usually in the form of routine reports. Often what is lacking in this type of culture is the information flow across the organization at peer level in the different functions, who often need the same information as each other in order to perform their responsibilities effectively. The principles of the role culture can be shown diagrammatically as:

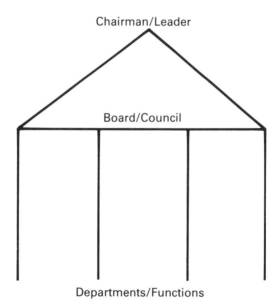

Figure 2.7
Role Culture

We can see quite clearly from the above paragraphs that there is no perfect management structure nor management culture to suit all organizations – they all vary according to the circumstances in which they find themselves. Sometimes the different structures and cultures co-exist within the same organization and, if organizations are to become and stay successful, they will need management information systems which can cope with these variations.

Types of Management Information System

In the previous section we have looked at the different types of management structures and cultures, and some of their different management information needs. As we stated earlier, the more complex the organization and the greater the diversity of different tasks carried out, the greater the need for management information. This need is then heightened if the organization is operating in an environment where a considerable degree of change is being experienced.

There are also one or two clear principles that operate in the development of a management information system. Generally, the more straightforward the structure and the culture, the more straightforward it is to work out the information needs and develop an overall MIS. Organizations where responsibilities are clearly defined and understood will also find it much easier to set up an effective MIS, as will those organizations where the structure and culture are not in conflict. In practice, it is a rare organization that achieves this and there will always be some blurring of the edges so far as managers' or departmental responsibilities are concerned. Indeed, some organizations which operate in a very dynamic environment adopt a *loose* style of organization structure to cope with their ever changing environment. So there will be a very different approach to the development of an MIS depending on whether the organization is highly structured or whether an informal, loose management structure or culture exists. The importance of an understanding of these different approaches will become clear, when we discuss in Chapter 3 how to set up and implement an MIS.

Let us now consider the traditional and probably most common organizational structure around, that based on functional lines, as shown in Figure 2.8. In the past, MIS's have tended to develop within each function. For example, the Director of Personnel might have under his/her control payroll and management information relating to all aspects of the staffing of the organization. The

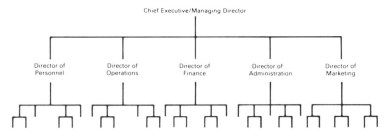

Figure 2.8
Traditional Hierarchical Structure

Director of Finance might have systems of budgetary control, information on the treasury function, etc. These systems will usually have been developed with only one purpose in mind – to suit their particular departmental or functional needs. So, they are known as *dedicated* systems, in that they are dedicated to one specific purpose and they will probably have been developed independently of each other. As the organization has grown both in size and complexity, so will the individual systems have grown and developed, often putting an almost impossible burden on an outdated computer system. Always assuming, that is, that there is *one* computer system in the organization – it is just as likely that, as the separate information needs have been identified, they will have been met by the development of information systems on different types of computer and computer programs. Many organizations are today ruing the detrimental effects of this type of sporadic MIS development on their efficiency and are staggered by the cost of conversion to a more corporate system covering all information needs.

So, what is the alternative to this *ad hoc* development of management information systems? The current favourite is the CORPORATE DATABASE system. Most of us have heard it mentioned and wondered what it means. In fact, it is very simple in concept and seemingly obvious in approach. It is made possible by the reduction in cost and increase in computer power available to most managers. The idea is that all the raw data on the organization is assembled in one vast common store, or database. (By raw data, we mean all the basic data about the organization, its markets, its staff and customers, its finances, etc., without any analysis or

evaluation of that data.) Managers' individual information requirements are satisfied from this database. The advantages of such an
approach are that:

a everyone is receiving information based on the same data – if
   a particular item is updated or changed it is automatically
   updated immediately on all the information systems using it;
b it is easy to change the base information and add to or delete
   from it without recourse to any major re-programming of the
   computer system;
c it is straightforward to set up information systems and then
   relatively easy to amend or adapt them;
d it more readily enables the use of request reports;
e it is usually very flexible and can allow managers to develop
   their own reporting systems.

So what we have here is a system which is very flexible. It is
admirably suited to an environment where change is the order of the
day. It is also 'tailor made' to take advantage of the technological
advantages of networked computer terminals (see Chapter 14)
which allow managers to have direct access to *their* computer and
hence directly into *their* MIS.

We have discussed here the two basic types of management
information systems:

a the one consisting of a collection of independent, dedicated
   systems, and
b the corporate database.

Some authors talk in terms of different types of MIS relating to
organizational activities such as stock control, payroll, etc., and
the systems used for decision making. We believe that these are
not different management information systems but merely different
branches of the type of functional system described above. The
real distinction between different types of management information
systems lies in whether they are the dedicated systems of the past
or the corporate database systems of the future.

Conclusion

In this chapter we have looked at how the structure and culture of the organization can affect the content and form of the management information system. We have seen how the more traditional, dedicated information systems are giving way to the more flexible and robust database systems. In the next chapter we give a brief outline of how a management information system might be developed and consider some of the practical, financial and human implications of implementing an MIS.

References

1　STONICH P J. *Implementing Strategy* (Ballinger, 1982).
2　HANDY C B. *Understanding Organizations* (Penguin, 1976).

3

Design and Implementation

Introduction

Designing and implementing management information systems in large organizations tends to be a major and complex activity and nowadays is the province of the specialist. So we may ask 'What do I need to know about it?' The simple answer is that it is too important *to us* to leave to the specialist. As a manager, or a professional in our own right, we will be the user of the MIS and will want to make sure that it is designed to meet *our* needs. The best way to ensure this is to understand the process so that our contribution can be both pertinent and timely. Without this level of understanding, many managers can be so put off by the thought of an MIS that they shy away from any involvement in its development. This can be a fatal mistake because all too often the specialist will be only too keen to implement their vision of the system. Consultation with all the parties is essential but requires hard work and co-operation on all sides.

One other thought is that any of us could find ourselves in the position of having to develop a small, simple MIS – perhaps designed particularly for our area of responsibility, say, a personnel system. The following steps and guidelines are as relevant to designing a small and simple MIS as they are to a large and complex system.

Design of a Management Information System

We advocate a systematic approach to the design of an MIS and to that end we believe that there is a logical order in which the various elements have to be tackled in order to ensure that there is a decent chance of ending up with a system that actually makes life easier rather than more difficult. This is not to say that local circumstances will not dictate some variation on this process, but being systematic actually improves the odds in favour of our success. With this in mind we have set out below the stages that we believe need to be followed in the design stage of an MIS:

a objectives and scope of the MIS;
b systems analysis;
c detailed specification;
d choice of software;
e choice of hardware;
f setting up the system.

Objectives and scope of the MIS. In order for the system designer to be able to set the project on the right course, it is essential that top management sets out clearly and definitively the *purpose* of the management information system. The key first questions are:

a What are we trying to achieve as a result of implementing the MIS?
b What management information needs are we trying to meet?
c Which parts of the organization will we include?
d What timescale will we be working to?

Systems analysis. Systems analysis can be a jargon term but in our context we take it to mean the process by which a business problem, in this case the design of an MIS, is addressed in a systematic way. This analysis will convert the overall objectives of the MIS into specific targeted requirements and will determine the overall structure of the system. It will tackle the issue of whether or not the MIS should be a manual or a computerized process. For the purpose of this chapter, we are going to assume that the decision is to computerize, although many of the following steps would apply equally well to a manual system. Another important issue at this stage, if the MIS is computerized, is whether the output will be paper-based or whether all managers will have access to their own computer terminals, or a combination of both.

Detailed specification. We have now arrived at a point where we have decided on the overall structure but have yet to choose our software and hardware. The next stage is a vital one – the detailed specification of the management information requirements. It is very tempting for the experts on the project team designing the MIS to decide that they know best and that the simplest approach is to produce the management information reports and then ask the managers or the other professionals to comment on them. This approach is fraught with dangers! Apart from probably not winning the commitment of the other managers to using and supporting the MIS, it is approaching the problem from the wrong direction. The right approach is to spend as much time as it takes with the potential users, asking them about their information needs. The interviewing skills of the system designers will have to be of the highest order and many use well designed questionnaires to assist them in this process. They will cover the key areas of:

a   what the manager does and what his/her responsibilities are;
b   what decisions the manager makes, that is, for what purposes the manager requires information;
c   what is the most useful form for the information to be presented to the manager;
d   how often, and when, the manager needs the information.

The task of the project team is to take the results of this research and these consultations and turn them into the management information system. Often the process will require frequent returns to the managers to clarify points and to test out ideas and reports. *The closer the involvement of the users of the MIS in its design, the better the final system will be.*

It can be hard work and sometimes very frustrating. Many managers will be initially unclear on what information they need, even supposing they are perfectly clear as to what are their exact responsibilities! Many potential users will have difficulty in seeing the usefulness and/or the relevance of the MIS and, in any case, will probably change their minds on their requirements as the system review proceeds! Our experience is that this is par for the course and it is vital that sufficient time and other resources are devoted to getting this stage right.

Choice of software. The next stage is the choice of SOFTWARE, that is, the computer programs. There will be a number of MIS software packages on the market and we will usually have three main options:

a   to use a standard, pre-designed package;
b   to use a standard, pre-designed package with adaptations to cope with the particular needs of our MIS. These adaptations can often be made for us by the software designers or, alternatively, they may be tackled by consultants or our own computer staff;
c   to design our own MIS computer system from scratch, specifically tailored to our needs.

In practice, the second option is the one most often used. It is rare that a standard MIS package will meet completely an individual organization's needs and considerable problems can occur if you try to force your information requirement to fit the package. However, this is a common mistake! The third option is usually very expensive although, done properly, it can ensure that the system design actually does match the information needs. The second option is a compromise, which generally works well. However, the choice of the package is still very important as too many alterations and adaptations to the original can be expensive and may well prejudice the overall robustness of the system.

Choice of hardware. Examples of the HARDWARE in this context are the computer itself and its associated peripherals, the visual display unit (the screen), the disk-drive, the printer, etc. The overall size of the proposed system and the choice of software will usually dictate the type of hardware chosen. The decision as to whether the output from the MIS will be paper based or from networked terminals will also be an important factor in the choice. Computer hardware and networking are discussed in more detail in Chapter 14.

Setting up the system. By now the system designers will have a pretty good idea of what information is required. The final stage in the design is to bring together all the disparate requirements of the users into a total system which will have the following principal attributes:

a   it will provide each manager with the information s/he requires, in the right form and at the right time;

b   the distribution of the information, be it paper based or computer networked, will be carried out efficiently and be trouble free. There is nothing worse than finding that our important report has been held up because the van delivering it has broken down or the computer system has hiccoughed and lost it somewhere;

c   the system should be sufficiently robust to meet changing needs. It is rare that an MIS will continue to meet the information needs of an organization indefinitely. In fact, in today's world of rapid change, an MIS should not be seen as *set* or *fixed* but as a system which may be constantly requiring change and adaptation. Hence it is vital that it is set up to allow these changes to happen without serious problems or difficulties. There are few things more frustrating to managers, whose information needs have changed and who know that changes are required to the system, to be told either that the changes are impossible, or prohibitively expensive, or can only be undertaken months or years ahead because of the workload on the computer or its human attendants. Database systems have the enormous advantage that they are generally more flexible and changes can be implemented relatively easily;

d   ideally, the system should be sufficiently USER FRIENDLY to allow the manager to make efficient and effective use of it. There is no point having a system which is so difficult to use that most managers will try to avoid it. Especially so if, when they do use it, they find it a time consuming and stressful experience.

We have now reached the final and exciting stage of implementing the system. We may think that we have done the difficult bit and the rest is plain sailing. Far from it, many an MIS has foundered during the implementation phase, so read on.

Implementation

There are two major types of issues involved in implementing a management information system, the practical issues and the human issues. The practical issues are usually well researched, understood and taken into account in the design stages of the MIS. However, the human issues are the ones that are sometimes overlooked or are not perceived as important. We shall look at both of these issues in turn.

Practical Issues

As you read on we suspect that some of you are going to say that these are obvious points, indeed so obvious that we are surprised to see them covered in a textbook such as this. However, anyone who has been involved in the development of an MIS will tell you that it is sometimes the most obvious, practical issues that are forgotten. Frequently this is because they fall into the 'between two stools' syndrome, that is nobody believes it is their responsibility. Often, it is because of the tremendous pressure to introduce the MIS as quickly as possible that some of the detailed, but vital, aspects get overlooked. Let's have a look at some of these practical issues.

The Equipment/Hardware. Clearly the computer equipment will need a home. Often with a main-frame computer it is important that the room in which it is housed is kept at an appropriate temperature and humidity, and is kept relatively dust-free. Also, depending on the size of the installation there may be special requirements for dealing with fire risks, for example, the use of a special inert gas system in the event of a fire.

If there are going to be several terminals made available to users, it will be important to decide at an early stage exactly where are the best locations. Although new offices are built with communication ducts to carry wiring around them, many of us will work for some time in buildings where the installation of another cable run is a major disturbance. In many circumstances it will be better, at the outset, to provide a network with more outlet points than can readily be used at the present, rather than have to make an expensive return visit after a few weeks and lay some more cable or move an outlet point. In any case the installation of such networks will be expensive and intrusive so it is imperative to start with a good plan.

Also, thought has to be given to such mundane issues as the furniture that the computers or terminals will sit on. Do busy managers have any space on their overcrowded desks to take a terminal and possibly a printer? Is the desk constructed in such a way as to reduce or contribute to problems of static electricity and vibration? What about static electricity? We only need to run a finger down the front of the TV set in the lounge in our home to recognize that static electricity is there. This can be a serious problem in a situation where sensitive data is being recorded on a magnetic storage medium, where the data can easily be corrupted by static electricity. There is also the question of where the visual display unit should be located relative to the light source in the room. We know about the problem of the reflection of light on our TV screens, how we have to strain our eyes at times to see the picture properly if there is a reflection on the screen, or a very bright source of light behind it. This problem is mutiplied many times over for a computer user who has to concentrate intently on the detailed characters on the computer screen for several hours a day. Finally, we need to be sure that the computer desks are suitable for the users. All of these problems can mean that it is necessary to have specially designed furniture to take the computer equipment and its cables in a safe way such that they are not a danger to staff and visitors. Ideally, there should be incorporated storage for computer disks, instruction books, manuals, etc., and a place for the printer and its associated reams of paper.

The timetabling of the installation, too, can be very tricky. You may be delighted to find out that the computer equipment is available at one month's notice and then realize that, for example, the furniture is available on a four month delivery schedule, or the cabling work will have to be done at the weekends to avoid disruption and will, therefore, take several months rather than the weeks envisaged. The lesson here is to plan! There is a variety of project planning tools available – the use of PERT-type networks for this purpose is discussed in Chapter 15.

Training. There can be a need for quite a major investment in training when a management information system is introduced. It will range from the type of specialist training required to look after the hardware and maintain the system, to the training required by the users, some of whom may be completely new to computers. This latter training, therefore, may often involve basic computer training as well as the training required to access and use the specific system installed. Also, we often find that it is not just, or only, the direct users that need this training but also support staff and top managers. Again, it is very important to plan the training so that it takes place at an optimum time. If it happens too early, much will have been forgotten before it is put into practice. At the other extreme, there is nothing more certain to ensure that an MIS gets off to a bad start than the system being in place and no-one properly trained to use it. In these circumstances the more interested or committed users will try to teach themselves, learning by trial and disaster, only to become frustrated, blaming the system for faults it does not have. Others will get used to having the hardware around, standing idle and just not being used.

People Issues

We have dealt with training as a practical issue, as indeed it is. However, we could just as easily have covered it under people issues. One of the greatest psychological problems concerning a new computerized MIS is that of fear. Fear of the unknown, fear of not being able to cope, fear of looking ridiculous to our juniors and colleagues, fear that the computer is going to affect our health. Training can help to alleviate most of these fears. If the design of the MIS has been carried out properly, with the full involvement of all those concerned at every stage, there is a good chance that all these fears will prove groundless and the implementation of the system will cause few people problems. So let's look at a few of these issues in a little more detail.

One of the greatest problems is people's fear of the MIS itself. For the older user who has not grown up with the computer, there can be very real concern that they will not be able to cope with the new technology. This is clearly far more of a problem on a networked computer system than on a paper based system. Also, these users may be concerned about how they are going to use the information which is about to cascade from the printer. Some users may be concerned that others will now have ready access to information which they themselves previously had been the only ones directly privy to. A source of their power had been to whom and when they would make this information available. Now, not only would their subordinates be able to bypass them in pursuit of accurate, up to date information but, being computer literate, they would be able to manipulate the computer and the information itself to better effect than themselves. However, if they are involved in the development of the system as we advocate and given training appropriate to their needs this should help alleviate the problem. Nevertheless, human nature being what it is, it will probably not go away all together! Time must be devoted to this issue, because it will not disappear if it is not tackled.

The vital message at all times is that the MIS is there to help the manager and the professional. It is *not* there as a threat to their ability to carry out their duties; it is *not* there to over-burden them with masses of paper; it is *not* there to manipulate or control them in some way. These messages must also be communicated to the support staff who may also feel threatened by a system they do not understand. It is important that these uncertainties should be resolved long before the introduction of the MIS. If they are not, people are entitled to feel threatened and we deserve to have difficulty in introducing our wonderful new system.

How about the problem of fear about the computer affecting our health? We are glad to report that there seems to be no recognized public health source or health regulating body, at this time, that has accepted any link between radio, electrical or electronic emissions from the visual display units that are harmful to health. This is not to say that people operating computers for many hours per day do not feel any ill effects, but most authorities have put these computer induced ailments down to poor environments, poor heating/cooling, lighting or ventilation. You might ask 'What about those headaches that computer operators seem to develop?' In many cases the answer might lie in the need for an eyetest and the provision of spectacles or a new prescription for existing spectacles. Many employers are willing to provide financial support and time off with pay for medical examinations and eyetests connected with the installation of computers. In many installations protective aprons are provided to screen the operators from possible harmful emissions, or arrangements are made whereby those seriously worried about possible health hazards and who cannot be reassured to the contrary, for example pregnant women, are transferred to other suitable work for an agreed period of time.

Good staff relations are imperative to the successful implementation of any change and the introduction of a computerized MIS is no exception. If relations are bad between management and staff, far from helping matters, it could well make matters worse. We said earlier that there is a need to consult with and take users along with us at every stage in the design and implementation of the MIS. The same principle applies to all the staff, whether they are to be users of the system or not. Few things worry employees more than the installation of computer systems because, rightly or wrongly in the past, computerization has gone hand in hand with the loss of jobs. Proper procedures for joint consultation (whether we are unionized or not), briefing groups, or whatever, are an essential ingredient in the reduction or removal of many of the psychological problems surrounding the introduction of the MIS.

Conclusion

With all these possible pitfalls and problems it is all too easy to take a mechanistic approach to the introduction of the MIS, that is, to treat the exercise as simply reading items off a checklist. However, we cannot stress too strongly the need to be aware of all the technical and human implications and of the possible range of responses and reactions of people to the new system. The success of a management information system will depend entirely on the use to which we and our colleagues put it. It can be technically the best MIS in the world, but if the users do not perceive it as such or understand how to get the best from it, it will be a failure. If there are business or organizational opportunities that are missed as a result of this, then it could be a very expensive failure indeed.

Part 2

Introduction to Statistics

'Numbers into Information'

Statistics is essentially a collection of quantitative techniques which can help interpret and transform a mass of data into information for use by the manager in decision making. We have chosen those techniques that we feel will be most useful to the practising manager and tried to present them in a straightforward and understandable form.

The first chapters in this part of the book, Chapters 4, 5 and 6, cover what we call descriptive statistics. These are techniques that can be used to help us present information to our bosses, staff, colleagues, shareholders, etc., in a way which they will find most easy to understand. Chapter 7 contains some essential stepping stones to the next chapter. They may seem a little theoretical and, dare we say, heavy going! Please persevere because they are the gateway into the fascinating and very useful techniques of sampling and hypothesis testing which are covered in Chapters 8 and 9 respectively. Chapter 10 addresses the subjects of regression and correlation. Do not be put off by these technical terms – this chapter simply helps us to identify and understand relationships in our data. The following chapter, Chapter 11, as its title – Time Series and Forecasting – suggests is all about helping the manager to look into the future. Chapter 12 tells us all we need to know about those peculiar numbers – indices – and, finally, Chapter 13 introduces the reader to some helpful techniques for structuring the decision making process.

We hope that these chapters present the techniques in a way you find easy to understand and absorb. However, if a particular section seems a little more difficult, please do not give up but persevere. We promise you that none of it is too bad and we hope some of it you will enjoy.

43

Table of Statistical Techniques and Examples of their Uses

TECHNIQUE	USES
Tabulations	The essential first steps in any summary or analysis of data is structuring it in tabular form. Examples are analysis of salary surveys, production performance.
Diagrammatic and Graphical Methods	These describe how data can be presented in diagrammatic or graphical form. Useful for illustrating reports and presentations.
Numerical Methods	Used for summarizing and highlighting key aspects of information, for example, using averages or medians to compare costs.
Probability	Deals with uncertainty in decision making – for example, calculating the likely effect on profitability of investing in a new factory, the likelihood of a sales call being successful, a product being defective.
Sampling	Used to obtain data and information on a large population more quickly and at less cost than by surveying the whole population, for example, market research into people's voting intentions, customer attitude towards new products.
Hypothesis Testing	Used to test hypotheses about a population from a sample. For example, testing the specification of a product or the effect of an advertising campaign.
Regression and Correlation	These measure the existence and strength of relationships between different variables, for example whether staff absenteeism is related to age, production costs to factory size. They also enable us to describe the relationships using mathematical equations.
Time Series and Forecasting	These are techniques used to forecast future events, for example, level of sales, production, markets.
Index Numbers	These are a useful way to measure changes in time by presenting the data as a proportion or percentage of a base figure and are particularly useful in comparing unlike elements. Examples are comparing changes in sales against changes in staffing, changes in product performance in different industries.
Decision Theory	These are techniques which help to structure a decision making problem and can be used in a variety of situations, for example, investment decisions, new product decisions, medical decisions.

4

Tabulations

Introducton

Data, in its RAW form, often does not readily convey much information and, as business professionals and/or managers, information is what we need to make decisions which are appropriate to the circumstances and produce the outcomes we require from our intervention.

To illustrate what we mean, let us take a typical set of data (potential information) that you might come across. For ease of demonstration we have chosen a simple example:

Table 4.1

Salaries of Employees
in a Small Firm

Employee A	£11,000
B	£11,500
C	£10,500
D	£12,500
E	£11,500
F	£11,000
G	£12,500
H	£10,000
I	£11,000
J	£9,500
K	£9,000
L	£10,500
M	£11,000
N	£13,500
O	£11,500
P	£13,000
Q	£12,000
R	£12,000
S	£9,500
T	£10,000

What can we infer from the above table? Not a lot, other than the lowest salary is £9,000 and the highest is £13,500, and the other salaries are spread out higgledy-piggledy between the lowest and the highest in steps of £500. Indeed, we may ask why would we have bothered to set out data in this way anyway? Let us suppose for the moment that the reason is that we wish to establish whether or not the company is paying market rates for its employees. If this was the case we might start by setting out the facts in some sort of table, probably in the order in which it has come from the salaries records. The table used above has set out the salaries in alphabetical order of employee surname.

Arrays

One way in which we can start to get a feel for the information that is locked inside the data is to see how it is distributed between the highest and lowest salaries. To do this we set out the salaries in ascending order of value – forming an ARRAY in ascending order:

Table 4.2
*Salaries in an Array
of Ascending Order*

Employee K	£9,000
J	£9,500
S	£9,500
H	£10,000
T	£10,000
C	£10,500
L	£10,500
A	£11,000
F	£11,000
I	£11,000
M	£11,000
B	£11,500
E	£11,500
O	£11,500
Q	£12,000
R	£12,000
D	£12,500
G	£12,500
P	£13,000
N	£13,500

Frequency Distribution

Does this start to tell us anything more? Again, not a lot except that more people are paid at the £11,000 salary level than at any other. So, how can we summarize the data to give us more information? One such way is to prepare it as a FREQUENCY DISTRIBUTION, that is, by showing the number of employees at each salary level:

Table 4.3
Frequency Distribution of Salaries

Salary	Frequency
£9,000	1
£9,500	2
£10,000	2
£10,500	2
£11,000	4
£11,500	3
£12,000	2
£12,500	2
£13,000	1
£13,500	1
Total	20

This way of setting out the data is beginning to tell us, for example, how the most frequently occurring salaries 'bunch' around £11,000–£11,500. More people are paid £11,000 than any other salary and we could, if we wished, use this as a crude comparison with another employer to test the competitiveness of our pay rates. It would not be a very effective comparison because it would show the same result against an organization, for example, who paid no salary over £11,000 provided that their most 'popular' salary was £11,000.

Now, if there was a large number of salary points it might be helpful to group the salaries into salary bands, as shown in Table 4.4. It is important that the bands or classes do not leave gaps and do not overlap. The bands or classes should always be the same size, unless this proves difficult as it sometimes will at the extreme ends of a widely spread distribution.

Table 4.4
Grouped Salaries

Salary Band	Frequency
£9,000 – £9,999	3
£10,000 – £10,999	4
£11,000 – £11,999	7
£12,000 – £12,999	4
£13,000 – £13,999	2
Total	20

Relative Frequency Distribution

Are we now at the stage where we can start to compare our salary levels with those of another organization? We could lay out or group their salaries as we have our own. If we do, what happens if the other organization, as is quite likely, has a different number of employees? The way to tackle this situation is to look at the percentages of the total number of employees in each organization at certain salary points or in salary bands. In this way we would produce a RELATIVE FREQUENCY DISTRIBUTION. Taking our two previous tables:

Table 4.5
Relative Frequency Distribution of Salaries

Salary	Frequency	%	Salary Band	Frequency	%
£9,000	1	5	£9,000 – £9,999	3	15
£9,500	2	10	£10,000 – £10,999	4	20
£10,000	2	10	£11,000 – £11,999	7	35
£10,500	2	10	£12,000 – £12,999	4	20
£11,000	4	20	£13,000 – £13,999	2	10
£11,500	3	15	Total	20	100
£12,000	2	10			
£12,500	2	10			
£13,000	1	5			
£13,500	1	5			
Total	20	100			

If we look at the grouped data, that is in salary bands, we can easily see that about one third of the employees

(15% + 20% = 35%) are paid in the range £9,000–£10,999, about one third (35%) are paid in the range £11,000–£11,999 and about one third (20% + 10% = 30%) are paid in the range £12,000–£13,999. We can now make the comparison between our organization and our competitor(s) in terms of what percentages of their employees fall into the various bands. The answer will give us information on our competitiveness.

Cumulative Frequency Distribution

Sometimes it might be helpful to know how many employees earn more than or less than a certain amount and express our comparison with another organization in these terms. In order to do this we would produce a CUMULATIVE FREQUENCY DISTRIBUTION as shown below for the grouped salaries used in our previous example:

Table 4.6
Cumulative Frequency Distribution of Salaries

Salary Band	Cumulative Frequency	Cumulative %
Less than or equal to £9,999	3	15
Less than or equal to £10,999	7	35
Less than or equal to £11,999	14	70
Less than or equal to £12,999	18	90
Less than or equal to £13,999	20	100

The cumulative frequency or cumulative percentage shows that 15% of the employees earn less than £10,000 or, alternatively, 85% (100% − 15%) earn £10,000 or more. Thirty-five per cent earn less than £11,000, 70% earn less than £12,000 and so on. Now we have a good basis on which to make some sort of a comparison of this organization's salary structure with that of other organizations.

You are now probably keen to get on to the next chapter and to get into the *real* statistics, but let us try the following example before you do so.

Example

Set out below is some data on the ages of employees in a small organization. What information can be drawn from the data?

Ages of employees:

25	56	22	53	21	30	30	18	39	43
32	42	35	41	29	35	39	32	37	47
29	38	46	36	17	22	24	16	27	37
35	29	62	34						

Where do we start? We could work out the average but, as yet, we do not know what the *average* means (we will cover averages in Chapter 6). Until then we stay with the methods we have discussed already.

Our first approach, again, is to set out a table showing the ages in an array of ascending order of magnitude:

16	17	18	21	22	22	24	25	27	29
29	29	30	30	32	32	34	35	35	35
36	37	37	38	39	39	41	42	43	46
47	53	56	62						

We can then go on to group the data in age ranges, say, with five-year intervals, and show the grouped frequency distribution, the relative frequency distribution and the cumulative frequency distribution (see Table 4.7).

Now we can beging to understand what the data might actually mean to the organization. From this table, only three of our staff are going to retire during the next 15 years. If these are managers, what are the implications of this for the organization's Succession Plan? We do not have the problem of a concentration of retirements, possibly leaving the organization short of experienced people. Instead, we might have the problem, if the future top management team is currently in the 30–34 and 35–39 age groups (some 40% of the employees fall in these groups), that they are going to suffer some serious career progression limitations if their career advancement is restricted by bottlenecks.

Unless something is done to prevent frustration from driving these up-and-coming middle managers to seek advancement by

Table 4.7

Employee Ages – Relative and Cumulative Frequency Distribution

Ages	No. of Employees in Age Group	Relative Frequency %	Cumulative Frequency %
Under 20	3	8.8	8.8
20 – 24	4	11.8	20.6
25 – 29	5	14.7	35.3
30 – 34	5	14.7	50.0
35 – 39	9	26.5	76.5
40 – 44	3	8.8	85.3
45 – 49	2	5.9	91.2
50 – 54	1	2.9	94.1
55 – 59	1	2.9	97.0
60 – 64	1	2.9	99.9*
	34	99.9*	

*varies from 100% due to rounding

moving to other organizations there could well be a significant incidence of staff turnover within the middle grades in the not-too-distant future. The intelligent analysis of the age profile may be the first early warning signals that this might be about to occur. Here is an example of the opportunity for the personnel professional to get in early to influence what is happening, rather than being left only to react to the crisis after the event.

Another interesting point to come from the cumulative frequency table is that 35% of the staff are under 30 years of age, 50% under 35 and 77% under 40 – quite a young age profile. What implications might this have for, say, the development of a new benefits package? They might be more interested in bonus payments than in pension provision. Whatever our decision on that subject, the information could not have been gleaned from the raw data on ages. So, we set off from a jumble of numbers and out of that has come management information.

Conclusion

In this chapter we have looked at ways in which raw data can be converted into meaningful information by setting it out in tabular form in arrays and frequency distributions. By using the relative and the cumulative forms of the distributions we continue the process of converting our raw data into information. It is only when we have carried out our analysis that the information is brought to light. In the next chapter we go on to look at other ways in which we can present our data so that it contributes to our decision making process.

5

Diagrammatic and Graphical Methods

Introduction

So far we have discussed organizing the data into tabular form and seen the benefits of this type of presentation. However, while we have used tabular methods in Chapter 4 to analyse the data, some people find it easier to understand information displayed in diagrammatic or graphical form.

Bar Diagram

The simplest technique is the BAR DIAGRAM. Let's look at an example of the use of a bar diagram in a sales situation. Suppose that there are three sales staff and the Sales Manager wants to keep a check on their progress. The Sales Manager can compile his monthly sales figures on a tabular basis as shown below with the actual sales listed per month and the relative sales per sales person as a percentage of the monthly total:

Table 5.1
Sales Performance

	January		February		March		Quarterly
	Sales	*%*	*Sales*	*%*	*Sales*	*%*	*Total*
Brown	£10,000	32	£12,000	24	£18,000	17	£40,000
Jones	£9,000	29	£18,000	36	£50,000	46	£77,000
Smith	£12,000	39	£20,000	40	£40,000	37	£72,000
Month Total	£31,000	100	£50,000	100	£108,000	100	£189,000

What does this tell the Sales Manager? Sales are obviously rising sharply month by month but who is actually scoring with the

53

customers. Let's see what happens when we set out these figures in the form of a bar diagram:

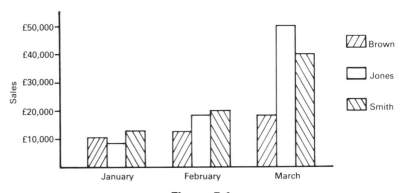

Figure 5.1
Bar Diagram showing Monthly Sales

From this picture we can easily see that Brown's progress is modest, Smith's results are very good while Jones' results are quite spectacular, starting from the lowest base of £9,000 in February to achieving the highest sales total of £50,000 in March.

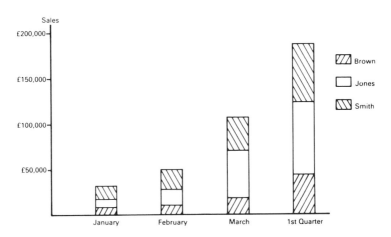

Figure 5.2
Stacked Bar Diagram showing Monthly 1st Quarter Sales

In a development of the bar diagram principle we could show the monthly sales totals by way of a stacked bar diagram, that is one in which the monthly sales of Brown, Smith and Jones are added together and distinguished by colour or different shading, as shown in Figure 5.2. This has the advantage that it shows the total increase in sales as well.

Pie Charts

Another useful way of depicting the sales information in a relative sense, that is to show pictorially the relative merits of the sales figures of Brown, Smith and Jones, is by use of a PIE CHART. As the name suggests, the total sales are shown as a circle with the sizes of the slices depicting the values of sales for the three staff, as shown in Figure 5.3.

Note how the area of the pie reflects the size of the total sales for the month, whereas the area/size of the slice equates to the proportion of total sales achieved by each sales person. In this way, we see at a glance that Jones is actually achieving a rising proportion of a growing monthly sales total.

Pictograms

One of the really eye catching ways of presenting statistics is by using pictures instead of bars in our bar diagrams. This is called a PICTOGRAM. Let's look at some examples:

a   Suppose we want to show growth in the sales of our company over a period of time. A picture we might use is the £ sign:

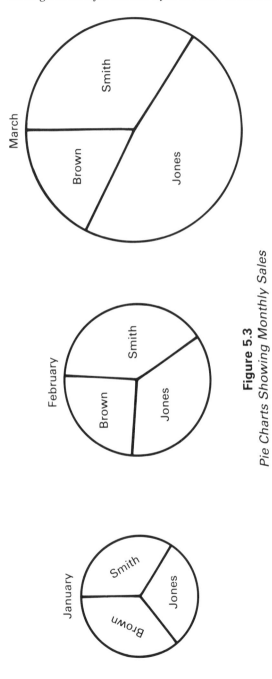

Figure 5.3
Pie Charts Showing Monthly Sales

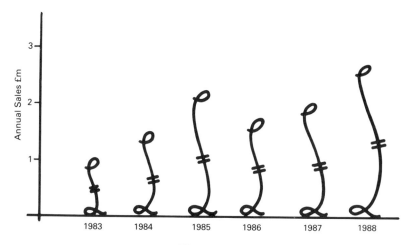

Figure 5.4
Pictogram showing Sales

b Suppose we want to demonstrate the change in numbers of employees over a period of time. Here the picture we might use is the stickperson:

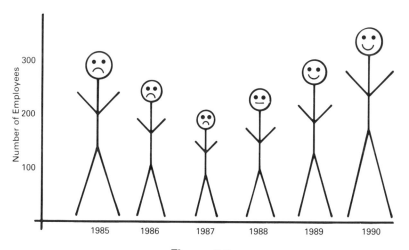

Figure 5.5
Pictogram showing Changes in Staffing

c   Suppose we are a local authority and we want to show how the money we collected was spent on council services. Here we might use bags of money as our pictorial representation:

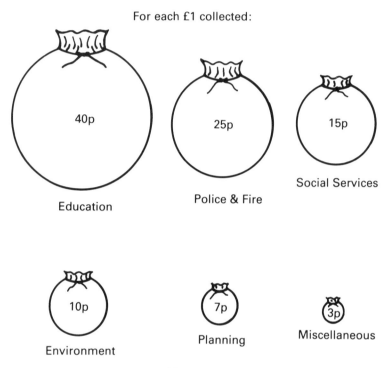

Figure 5.6
Pictogram showing Allocation of Income to Services

As you will see from Figures 5.4 and 5.5, the heights of the pictures represent the numbers involved and are equivalent to the heights of the bars in a bar diagram. In Figure 5.6 it is the area of the bag (rather like the area of a pie chart) which provides the scale for comparison. It is most important to ensure that the dimensions we have used for comparison are made clear to the reader. With pictograms, there is endless scope for us to use our imagination to provide good *visuals* to help get our message across to our audience of professional and management colleagues. It is also of particular use when we are trying to communicate with a wider audience, some of whom may not have a good understanding of the more sophisticated graphical and diagrammatic methods. A good example of the latter is the summary version of Company Annual Report and Accounts produced by large companies for the benefit of their shareholders. However, when producing our pictograms we do need to take care in judging what the audience would find appropriate to their needs.

Histogram

One of the best ways of representing a frequency distribution is by means of a HISTOGRAM. Take the following set of data about daily sales of bread from a bakery (each unit of sale is 10 kilograms):

Table 5.2
Daily Bread Sales

Week	Day 1	Day 2	Day 3	Day 4	Day 5	Day 6
1	69	70	73	70	71	71
2	67	72	71	71	68	73
3	67	70	74	68	70	70
4	66	68	67	70	69	69
5	68	70	72	73	72	71
6	70	69	69	72	70	73
7	66	70	72	73	74	68
8	70	70	73	68	66	67
9	71	65	68	70	72	70
10	70	70	68	74	72	71

Once again the raw data does not give us very much useful management information, in fact it is a quite meaningless jumble of figures in its present form. However, we can start to make sense of the data by going through the process described in Chapter 4 and first setting out the data in an array of ascending order. From this we can produce a frequency distribution listing all the days of '65' sales (that is, 1), then all the days of '66' sales (3), then all the days of '67' sales (4), and so on to all the days of '74' sales (3), as shown in Table 5.3:

Table 5.3
Frequency Distribution of Daily Bread Sales

Daily Sales	Frequency of Occurrence
65	1
66	3
67	4
68	8
69	5
70	16
71	7
72	7
73	6
74	3
	60

By setting out Table 5.3 in the form of a bar diagram of frequency against daily sales we get our histogram:

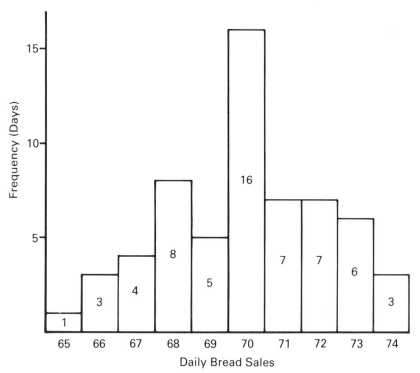

Figure 5.7
Histogram showing Daily Bread Sales

Our histogram shows the frequency of daily sales and we can see that the tops of the columns form a sort of graph, rising in the middle and tailing off at both ends. Even now the information is still not leaping out of the page at us, although by inspection you can see that '70' sales occur more often than the other sales, and sales seem to be fairly evenly spread above and below the '70' figure.

How can we take the presentation a step further? Statisticians use the technique previously mentioned of grouping the data. Let us see what happens to our histogram when we group '65' sales with '66' sales, '67' sales with '68' sales, etc., and in addition present our information as relative frequencies, that is, percentages of the total. The information in tabular form is set out below in Table 5.4. We have to think a little at this stage about the group or class boundaries. Sometimes the real boundaries are the midpoints between the top of the previous class and the bottom of the next class. However, in our table below, the real boundaries are 64, 66, 68, 70, 72 and 74. When we come to draw our histogram

Table 5.4
Relative Frequency Distribution of
Grouped Daily Bread Sales

Grouped Daily Sales	Frequency	Relative Frequency %
65 – 66	4	7
67 – 68	12	20
69 – 70	21	35
71 – 72	14	23
73 – 74	9	15
	60	100

it is sometimes easier just to show classes and at other times to show the real boundaries. In the histogram in Figure 5.8 we have shown both to emphasize this point.

You may be forgiven at this stage for asking what practical significance all the above might have. Well, imagine you are a manager of the department or shop which has produced the sales data that we have been working on. Assuming that your requirements for sales staff bear some relationship to the sales

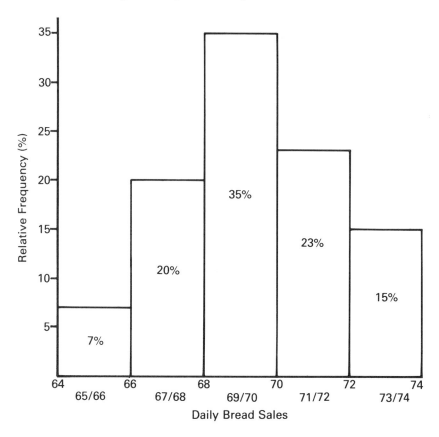

Figure 5.8
Histogram showing Grouped Daily Bread Sales

volumes each day, you could get an indication of the 'right' level of staffing from this exercise. From our grouped data histogram we can see that '65' to '68' sales occurred on 27% of the days; '69' to '70' sales occurred on 35% of the days; and '71' to '74' sales occurred on 38% of the days. As it is often unpredictable as to which are the busy sales days and which are the quiet ones and also unlikely that the manager will be able to employ casual staff at short notice on the busy days, then the grouped data histogram would be of some help. By staffing up to the '69' to '70' sales days his staff levels would be correct for 35% of the time. For 27% of the time the shop would be overstaffed and 38% of the time it would be understaffed – very approximately one third of the sales days falling into each category.

By the way, the data in a graph or histogram which rises to about the middle then slopes off at about the same rate as it rose, as in our grouped data histogram, is said to have a symmetric distribution and something approaching the celebrated NORMAL DISTRIBUTION. Statisticians love a normal distribution because it allows them to make assumptions about the way the data will behave in their calculations. We will examine the normal distribution in Chapter 7.

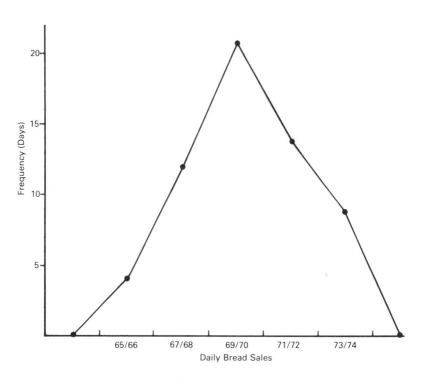

Figure 5.9
Frequency Polygon showing Grouped Daily Bread Sales

Frequency Polygon

Another way of displaying the data from a histogram, which some people find more helpful, is to show it as a FREQUENCY POLYGON. Here, instead of using bars to show the frequency of events we plot a graph of points at heights corresponding to the frequencies. Where the data is grouped the points plotted are the group frequencies and are shown above the mid-point of the group intervals, as in Figure 5.9. In order for our frequency polygon to touch the horizontal (*x* axis) we have added groups of zero frequency at both ends of the graph.

Ogive

Our final graphical/diagrammatic method is to plot a graph of the cumulative frequency distribution. This is called an OGIVE and here the cumulative frequencies (of bread sales in our example) are plotted on the vertical axis (that is, the *y* axis) and the bread sales units along the *x* axis. The ogive can be particularly helpful to us in a situation where it is useful to know, for example in our bread sales situation above, the number of days when the sales of bread is equal to or less than a particular figure. We are easily able to draw up a table showing the cumulative frequencies from Table 5.5:

Table 5.5
Cumulative Frequency Distribution of
Grouped Daily Bread Sales

Grouped Bread Sales	Cumulative Frequency
Less than or equal to 66 units	4
Less than or equal to 68 units	16
Less than or equal to 70 units	37
Less than or equal to 72 units	51
Less than or equal to 74 units	60

To plot an ogive, the cumulative frequency is drawn against the upper boundary of each class, for example, 4 is plotted against 66 on the x-axis, 16 is plotted against 68 on the x-axis, etc. The zero point of our ogive is shown at the lowest real boundary, that is, 64. Our ogive would then look like this:

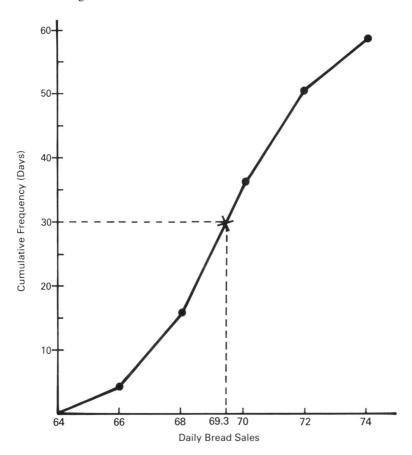

Figure 5.10
Ogive showing Cumulative Frequency of Daily Bread Sales

Coming back to our staffing example in the bakery, if our manager knew that his staff could cope with up to 70 units of bread sales per day he could tell from the cumulative frequency table or the ogive that they would cope on 37 out of the 60 days. The usefulness of the ogive is that it allows readings from intermediate points, for example, if the manager wanted to increase staff to be able to cope with sales on half of the days, s/he could read across the ogive curve from the cumulative frequency of 30 to give a result of 69.3. Therefore if s/he increased staff to deal with daily bread sales of 69 units, then for about half of the time the shop would cope. This is a particularly useful facility if the groupings are larger than those used in our example. Of course, the intermediate points could have been worked out from the table, but it is a lot easier to read off from a graph and certainly easier to communicate from this particular picture in, say, a presentation to management colleagues.

Conclusion

We hope we have demonstrated how the picture, by way of diagrammatic and graphical methods, can paint a thousand words. We have covered the bar diagram, pie chart, pictogram, histogram, frequency polygon and ogive, showing how easy it is to present the data in these ways. In the next chapter we go on to look at the ways in which numerical methods can be used to help provide management information to the decision makers.

6

Numerical Methods

Introduction

So far, so good, but what about all the figure work that statistics is supposed to be about? What about all the calculations and formulae with all those Greek letters that are so confusing to the non-statistician? Well, in Chapters 4 and 5 we covered ways of presenting and summarizing data using tables and then diagrams and graphs. Both these methods are very useful in illustrating points you may wish to make in a report or as visual aids in a presentation. However, numerical methods are sometimes very effective in summarizing data and become particularly valuable when the data is a sample from which you wish to draw inferences about the overall population.

There are usually two aspects of a DATA SET in which we will be interested. The most common are indications of the middle or *average* value of the data set – referred to as MEASURES OF LOCATION. The second type are concerned with the extent to which the data is spread around the middle or average value – referred to as MEASURES OF DISPERSION.

Measures of location

There are three main measures of location with which you will need to become familiar – the mean (sometimes called the arithmetic mean or average), the median and the mode. The first is probably the most widely used.

The MEAN is obtained by adding together all the individual items of data and then dividing by the number of items in the data set. Let us look at a simple extract from one of our earlier examples. Do you remember about the monthly sales figures of Brown, Jones and Smith? Here are their January sales figures again to remind you:

Table 6.1
Sales Performance for January

Brown	£10,000
Jones	£9,000
Smith	£12,000
Month Total	£31,000

Some organizations measure the performance of their salesforce by comparing individual monthly sales figures with the mean for all the sales people. The mean of the January sales figures is obtained by adding up the totals for each sales person and dividing by the number of data items. In this case there are three sales persons, so we divide the total by three to get a mean of £10,333.

The Statisticians have a beautiful way of complicating this simple principle. They say, let $x_1, x_2, \cdots x_n$ be the individual values of a data set with n points in it, then the mean is calculated by the following formula:

$$\text{mean} = \frac{x_1 + x_2 \ldots + x_n}{n}$$

A mathematical notation which is commonly used by the statisticians to indicate 'the sum of' individual data items is the Greek letter Σ (capital sigma), so

$$\sum_{i=1}^{n} x_i$$

means the sum of the values of x from x_1 up to x_n, where the subscript (1) and superscript (n) denote the range over which the data is summed. In other words,

$$\sum_{i=1}^{n} x_i = x_1 + x_2 + \cdots + x_i \cdots + x_n,$$

and the mean, therefore $= \sum_{i=1}^{n} \frac{x_i}{n}$

Here we must pause for a moment and introduce the concept of a *population* and a *sample*. A POPULATION is defined as being a collection of all items in which we are interested. For example, if we were marketing managers interested in promoting the sales of cosmetics in the UK, our population of interest could be all women in the UK over the age of 14. Alternatively, the production manager in a factory making radios could be interested in quality control. His/her population here would be the total production of radios. A SAMPLE is a portion of the population selected to represent the whole. Going back to our examples, we might choose a sample of, say, 500 women aged over 14 and find out what cosmetics they use. Our production manager might choose a sample of, say, 100 radios and test to see how many were defective. We would then use the results from our sample to tell us about the population as a whole.

We will return to the fascinating subject of sampling in Chapter 8. However, it is important to come to grips with some conventions at this stage. The mean of a population (with N values) is usually referred to by the Greek letter 'mu', written μ. The mean of a sample (with n values) is represented by the symbol $\bar{x}$ (called 'x bar'). The means for a population and a sample are calculated using the same formula – that shown in the previous paragraph.

Let us take another example. Perhaps these statisticians have not complicated things at all with their formulae because we can now see what happens when we substitute the data from the next example into our formula to derive the mean from this data set:

We have the following sales figures for a company over a period of twelve years (our population in this case). What is the mean (average) sales for the period?

Table 6.2
Company Sales

Year	Sales (£000)	Year	Sales (£000)
1	100	7	250
2	200	8	200
3	250	9	100
4	300	10	250
5	250	11	300
6	150	12	150

Substituting this data into our formula we have:

$$\text{mean, } \mu = \sum_{i=1}^{12} \frac{x_i}{n}$$

$$= \frac{x_1 + x_2 + x_3 + x_4 + x_5 + x_6 + x_7 + x_8 + x_9 + x_{10} + x_{11} + x_{12}}{12 \text{ (the number of years)}}$$

$$= \frac{2,500}{12}$$

$$= 208.333$$

Therefore the average sales per year is £208,333.

The average or mean is a familiar concept to most of us. We can use it, if we wish, following on from our previous example, to compare the sales of two or more different products over a period of time. The mean sales over the period could be a useful indicator of which product was performing the best over the period. Although we have used sales as the basis for our example, in fact the range of applications is infinite, for example, salaries, production levels, costs, etc.

The mean is a useful way of comparing two sets of data provided that the data has a symmetric distribution. If the distribution of the data is not symmetric but is bunched up at one end or the other, it is said to be SKEWED. When data is skewed it is helpful to use another measure of location, the median, to help with our comparison.

The MEDIAN is probably the second most commonly used measure of location after the mean. It is the value falling in the middle when the data items are arranged in an array of either ascending or descending order. If there is an odd number of items, the median is the value of the middle item. If there is an even number of items, the median is obtained by calculating the mean of the two middle items.

Let us look at an example where, say, we have two machines that can each produce up to 100 units per day. Machine A runs regularly during the week, while Machine B breaks down frequently and produces fewer units on some days. The figures are for a sample week:

Table 6.3
Machine Production – Mean

	Machine A Production	Machine B Production
Monday	90	95
Tuesday	95	85
Wednesday	85	10
Thursday	90	90
Friday	85	90
Saturday	95	15
Sunday	90	95
Total	630	480
Mean, $\bar{x}$,	$\dfrac{630}{7}$	$\dfrac{480}{7}$
	= 90 per day	= 68.6 per day

We have worked out the mean and while this might be helpful in some respects, for example in the allocation of production overheads, it is fairly unhelpful in respect of staffing the department or section which has to cope with moving or storing finished goods on a daily basis. The mean figures would suggest that we would require some 31% more staff to cope with the output from Machine A than from Machine B. However, if we work out the median for each machine (see below) we note that this is 90 units per day in each case, causing us to look again at our staffing levels.

Table 6.4
Machine Production – Median

Machine A			Machine B
85			10
85			15
90			85
90	← Median →		90
90			90
95			95
95			95

We could also use this method to compare the competitiveness of the salaries of several organizations. Let us set out the salary data for each organization in an array of ascending order, as shown in Table 6.5.

Table 6.5
Comparison of Salary Data

Organization 1		Organization 2		Organization 3	
6,000		7,145		3,260	
6,475		7,300		3,365	
6,900		7,465		3,704	
7,125		7,533		5,703	
7,436	← Lower	8,400	← Lower	5,900	
8,500	quartile	8,950	quartile	6,104	
9,636	7,968	9,104	8,675	6,236	← Lower
9,700		9,636		7,000	quartile
10,500		9,745		7,124	6,236
10,900	Median	9,800		7,236	
11,500	← 11,200	10,115	← Median	7,438	
12,000		11,651	10,115	8,000	
12,265		11,832		8,200	Median
12,500		12,014		8,700	← 8,450
12,600	Upper	12,125		8,715	
12,600	← quartile	12,446	Upper	9,300	
13,000	12,600	12,608	← quartile	9,816	
13,700		13,032	12,527	10,230	
14,500		13,500		11,363	
17,343		13,700		12,140	← Upper
		13,950		12,500	quartile
				12,600	12,140
				12,716	
				12,999	
				13,200	
				14,600	

Using the median as a means of comparing the competitiveness of the three organization's salaries then Organization 1 with a median of 11,200 ((10,900 + 11,500) ÷ 2)) is the most attractive compared with 10,115 for Organization 2 and 8,450 for Organization 3. To refine this comparison further we can calculate the UPPER and LOWER QUARTILES and use these together with the medians to make further comparisons between the three organizations. The upper quartile is that value, in an array of numbers, above which one quarter of the values fall and three-quarters fall below. The lower quartile is the value, in an array, above which three-quarters of the values fall and one quarter of the numbers fall below. In this way, using the median, the upper quartile and the lower quartile we get three benchmarks with which to compare the salaries (or any other data we wish to compare) in the three organizations. In our example:

	Organization 1	*Organization 2*	*Organization 3*
Lower quartile	7,968	8,675	6,236
Median	11,200	10,115	8,450
Upper quartile	12,600	12,527	12,140

Does this tell us anything more? What it does show is that the salaries of Organization 2 are the best or most competitive at the lower levels (the lower quartile), the salaries of Organization 1 are the best at the middle levels, and, while Organization 1 and Organization 2 are both slightly more competitive than Organization 3, there is little to choose between them at the upper levels.

We can, if we wish, take this measure of location further, by looking at PERCENTILES and DECILES. Percentiles divide the range of data in the array into 100ths. In this way the median is the 50th percentile, the upper quartile in an ascending array is the 75th percentile and the lower quartile is the same as the 25th percentile. Deciles are simply percentiles ranged in groups of ten. The first decile in an ascending array has 10% of the values below it and 90% above it. The second decile has 20% of the values below it and 80% above it, and so on.

The third, and last, measure of location that we shall consider is the MODE. The mode is the term given to the value that occurs with the greatest frequency in our data set. In the bread sales example given in Chapter 5, the most commonly occurring daily sales unit is '70' with 16 occurrences, so this is the mode for that data set.

So, by use of the mean (average), median, quartiles, percentiles, deciles and mode we can compare the data on different organizations or machines or anything else we care to choose, and locate the benchmarks for our comparisons with as much precision as we like. One final thing to remember about the mean, median and the mode is that, when the distribution of the data is symmetric, they are the same for all practical purposes. It is only when the distribution is skewed that they differ.

Measures of dispersion

When we have obtained our data it is sometimes important to know how variable or dispersed the data values are. Take a simple example – you are a manufacturer and have a machine which is vital to your production process. You have a choice of two service agents, both of whom say that, on average, they will repair a machine breakdown in four hours. You have been caught by these vague statements before so, with the benefit of having read this book, you ask for evidence of their actual repair time for a sample of the most recent 20 call-outs. The data you receive is as follows:

Table 6.6
Repair Times

Agent A	Repair time	5,	4,	3,	4,	3,	5,	4,	4,	4,	5,
	(hours)	3,	4,	3,	3,	4,	4,	4,	5,	5,	4.
Agent B	Repair time	3,	4,	5,	5,	2,	7,	5,	4,	3,	5,
	(hours)	4,	2,	6,	4,	4,	5,	3,	4,	3,	2.

By substituting these values in our formula

$$\text{mean, } \bar{x}, = \sum_{i=1}^{n} \frac{x_i}{n}$$

we can calculate the mean for each data set at 4 hours – so neither agent is breaking the trades description legislation and we have nothing to choose between them. However, when we set out the data as one of our histograms (which plot values against the frequency with which they occur – see pages 59–63), the results are shown in Figures 6.1a and 6.1b.

Now we can begin to distinguish between the service provided by the two agents. While it may be useful to have our machine repaired in 2 hours on 15% of occasions it might be totally unacceptable to have to wait for 6 hours for 5% of the time and 7 hours for 5% of the time. So, Agent A is the one for us. It is the dispersion of the data that has allowed us to discriminate between the two agencies.

The simplest measure of dispersion is the RANGE. The range for a set of data is the arithmetic difference between the highest and

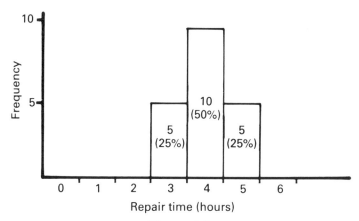

Figure 6.1a
Histogram of Repair Times for Agent A

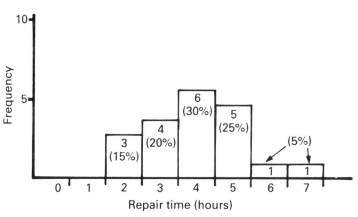

Figure 6.1b
Histogram of Repair Times for Agent B

the lowest value. In our example above, the range of repair times for Agent A is $5 - 3 = 2$. The range of repair times for Agent B is $7 - 2 = 5$. The data for Agent B is dispersed over a wider range than that of Agent A; however, apart from allowing us to decide which service best suits our needs, the significance of a wide or narrow range of data will be discussed later. We will come back to it in Chapter 8 when we cover sampling and the drawing of inferences.

The range is a perfectly adequate measure of dispersion for many purposes but falls down as a vehicle to assess our data when, for example, there are *rogue* values at the top or bottom of the range which are some distance removed from the other values. In these cases the measures of dispersion called the VARIANCE and STANDARD DEVIATION are much more reliable than the range.

Both of these are measures of how dispersed the data is about the mean. To calculate them we:

a   First find the mean of the data set by adding up all the values in the data set and dividing this by the number of values. For Agent A and Agent B above the mean is the same, $80 \div 20 = 4$.

b   Subtract each value from the mean to get the deviation from the mean.

c   Then square the deviations to get rid of the minus signs as we are only interested in the size of the deviation and not whether it is positive or negative.

d   Add together the squares and divide the sum by the number of values in the case of a population and by the number of values minus 1 for a sample. In our example we divide the sum by $20 - 1 = 19$, as it is a sample. We now have the variance of the data.

e   As we had previously squared the deviations to get rid of the minus sign we now have to take the square root to obtain the standard deviation.

Expressed as formulae, where $x_1 \cdots x_N$ are the values of the population and μ the population mean:

Variance of the population, usually referred to as σ^2,

$$= \sum_{i=1}^{N} \frac{(x_i - \mu)^2}{N}$$

Standard deviation of the population, referred to as σ,

$$= \sqrt{\sum_{i=1}^{N} \frac{(x_i - \mu)^2}{N}}$$

Similarly the formulae for a sample set, where $x_1 \cdots x_n$ are the values and $\bar{x}$ the sample mean:

Variance of the sample, usually referred to as s^2,

$$= \sum_{i=1}^{n} \frac{(x_i - \bar{x})^2}{n - 1}$$

Standard deviation of the sample, referred to as s,

$$= \sqrt{\sum_{i=1}^{n} \frac{(x_i - \bar{x})^2}{n - 1}}$$

Returning to our example, the calculations look like this:

Agent A Repair time (hours) 5, 4, 3, 4, 3, 5, 4, 4, 4, 5, 3, 4, 3, 3, 4, 4, 4, 5, 5, 4.

Agent B Repair time (hours) 3, 4, 5, 5, 2, 7, 5, 4, 3, 5, 4, 2, 6, 4, 4, 5, 3, 4, 3, 2.

A	Deviation From Mean	Deviation Squared	B	Deviation From Mean	Deviation Squared
5	−1	1	3	1	1
4	0	0	4	0	0
3	1	1	5	−1	1
4	0	0	5	−1	1
3	1	1	2	2	4
5	−1	1	7	−3	9
4	0	0	5	−1	1
4	0	0	4	0	0
4	0	0	3	1	1
5	−1	1	5	−1	1
3	1	1	4	0	0
4	0	0	2	2	4
3	1	1	6	−2	4
3	1	1	4	0	0
4	0	0	4	0	0
4	0	0	5	−1	1
4	0	0	3	1	1
5	−1	1	4	0	0
5	−1	1	3	1	1
4	0	0	2	2	4
80		10	80		34

Agent A   *Agent B*

$\bar{x} = \dfrac{80}{20} = 4$ $s^2 = \dfrac{10}{19}$ $\bar{x} = \dfrac{80}{20} = 4$ $s^2 = \dfrac{34}{19}$

$\phantom{\bar{x} = \dfrac{80}{20} = 4}$ $= 0.53$ $\phantom{\bar{x} = \dfrac{80}{20} = 4}$ $= 1.79$

$\phantom{\bar{x} = \dfrac{80}{20} = 4}$ $s = \sqrt{0.53}$ $\phantom{\bar{x} = \dfrac{80}{20} = 4}$ $s = \sqrt{1.79}$

$\phantom{\bar{x} = \dfrac{80}{20} = 4}$ $= 0.73$ $\phantom{\bar{x} = \dfrac{80}{20} = 4}$ $= 1.34$

Hence the standard deviation for A is 0.73 and 1.34 for B. So, the data on Agent B is about twice as dispersed as that for Agent A.

The earlier formulae can be simplified to the following, which is particularly useful when we have large data sets:

$$\sigma^2 = \frac{\sum\limits_{i=1}^{N} x_i^2 - \dfrac{\left(\sum\limits_{i=1}^{N} x_i\right)^2}{N}}{N}$$

$$\sigma^2 = \sqrt{\frac{\sum\limits_{i=1}^{N} x_i^2 - \dfrac{\left(\sum\limits_{i=1}^{N} x_i\right)^2}{N}}{N}}$$

$$s^2 = \frac{\sum\limits_{i=1}^{n} x_i^2 - \dfrac{\left(\sum\limits_{i=1}^{n} x_i\right)^2}{n}}{n-1}$$

$$s^2 = \sqrt{\frac{\sum\limits_{i=1}^{n} x_i^2 - \dfrac{\left(\sum\limits_{i=1}^{n} x_i\right)^2}{n}}{n-1}}$$

Using the simplified formula and the data from our example, our table of working would look like this:

A	A^2	B	B^2
5	25	3	9
4	16	4	16
3	9	5	25
4	16	5	25
3	9	2	4
5	25	7	49
4	16	5	25
4	16	4	16
4	16	3	9
5	25	5	25
3	9	4	16
4	16	2	4
3	9	6	36
3	9	4	16
4	16	4	16
4	16	5	25
4	16	3	9
5	25	4	16
5	25	3	9
4	16	2	4
$\Sigma A = 80$	$\Sigma A^2 = 330$	$\Sigma B = 80$	$\Sigma B^2 = 354$

$$\text{The standard deviation of A} = \sqrt{\frac{\Sigma A^2 - \dfrac{(\Sigma A)^2}{n}}{n-1}}$$

$$= \sqrt{\frac{330 - \dfrac{(80)^2}{20}}{19}}$$

$$= \sqrt{\frac{330 - 320}{19}}$$

$$= 0.73$$

$$\text{The standard deviation of B} = \sqrt{\frac{\Sigma B^2 - \dfrac{(\Sigma B)^2}{n}}{n-1}}$$

$$= \sqrt{\frac{354 - \frac{(80)^2}{20}}{19}}$$

$$= \sqrt{\frac{354 - 320}{19}}$$

$$= 1.34$$

You will see that the results of this simplified calculation are just the same as the ones on page 78.

The standard deviation will be put to further practical use when we come to Chapters 7 and 8 on probability and sampling. For now settle for the fact that the standard deviation is a measure of the extent to which our data is dispersed about the mean. In our example above, we could have come to the conclusion that B is more dispersed than A, simply by inspecting the data. However, when we have hundreds or thousands of items of data, or a large number of comparisons to be made, we need a calculation to reduce the problem to a single numerical value, hence our use of the standard deviation.

Conclusion

In this chapter we have started to get to grips with some number crunching and we have also met our first Greek letters. We have looked at measures of location (mean, median and mode) and measures of dispersion (range, variance and standard deviation) and seen how they can be used to compare different sets of data. We will see that the standard deviation is very useful in many statistical techniques and will return to it in several of the following chapters.

7

Probability and Probability Distributions

Introduction

PROBABILITY is a concept of vital importance to the manager and one which s/he will use knowingly or unknowingly almost every working day. A manager is faced all the time with the need to make decisions that involve uncertainty; why else is the manager so well paid? Situations regularly crop up such as:

a Should we invest in a new factory, and what is the likely effect on profitability?
b What is the likelihood that our employees will settle for a 7% wage increase?
c What is the likelihood that a price decrease will boost sales?

Probability is a measure of uncertainty, a measure of the chance or likelihood that a particular event may occur. It is expressed on a scale of 0 to 1. If the probability is close to 0 then the event is very unlikely to take place; if it is close to 1 then it is very likely to take place. If the probability is 0.5 then the event is equally likely or unlikely to take place.

Experiments and Outcomes

To get information on probabilities we carry out experiments or, in the business world, market research. Let us stay for a while with the concept of an experiment. An experiment will have outcomes and some examples are given overleaf:

Experiment	*Outcome*
Toss a coin	Head, tail
Throw a dice	1, 2, 3, 4, 5, 6
Make a sales call	Sale, no sale
Inspect a product	Perfect, imperfect

An outcome is often referred to as a SAMPLE POINT and all possible outcomes are the SAMPLE SPACE. Take the example of tossing the coin:

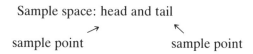

Sample space: head and tail

sample point   sample point

Now consider a more complex example, where we toss a coin twice. A graphical way to help us think about this is a TREE DIAGRAM:

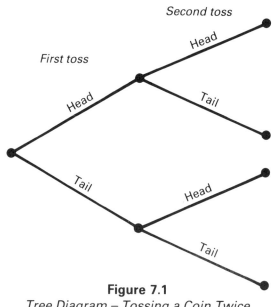

Figure 7.1
Tree Diagram – Tossing a Coin Twice

Outcomes, or sample points, of this experiment are:

head, head
head, tail
tail, head
tail, tail

These four sample points form the sample space.

The basic rules of probability are as follows:

a   probability values lie between 0 and 1;
b   the sum of all the probability values associated with the outcomes of an experiment must be 1.

Experimental Outcomes and their Probabilities

Associated with each experimental outcome is the probability of it occurring. There are three basic methods of assigning a probability to an experimental outcome:

a   the classical method;
b   the relative frequency method;
c   the subjective method.

The CLASSICAL METHOD is based on the assumption that each outcome is equally likely. Good examples of this are tossing a coin and throwing a dice. When tossing a coin the probability of getting a head or tail is equally likely and as there are only two possible outcomes the probability is 1/2, or 0.5, of getting a head or a tail. With the dice there are six outcomes, each equally likely. Therefore the probability of getting a particular number is 1/6, or 0.17. In our experiment of tossing a coin twice there are four outcomes and therefore the probability of getting a particular outcome is 1/4 or 0.25.

The RELATIVE FREQUENCY METHOD is based on conducting an experiment or test to assess probability values. For example, suppose you are testing a product to see if it is perfect or defective. Suppose we take a sample, say 100 items chosen at RANDOM, test them and find that 90 are perfect and 10 are defective. By random, we mean chosen such that every member of the population is equally likely to be a member of the sample, independently of which other members of the population are chosen (more of this in Chapter 8). The proportion of defective items in the sample is 10/100, or 0.1. If the ratio of defective to perfect items in the sample is the same as in the overall population then we could infer that the probability of finding defective items overall is 0.1.

The SUBJECTIVE METHOD is, as the name suggests, where you make a best guess, based on examining the available information. Thus, the probability of a horse winning a race might be assessed as 0.5 by one punter, but 0.4 by another reader of the form book. The subjective method reflects the individual's beliefs or expertise.

Events and their Probabilities

An EVENT is a collection of outcomes or sample points. For example, an event would be the probability of getting at least one head showing in two tosses of a coin. Looking back at our tree diagram on page 82 the event, obtaining at least one head, would include the following outcomes:

> head, head
> head, tail
> tail, head

but not tail, tail as this outcome contains no heads.

The probability of a particular event is equal to the sum of the probabilities of the sample points in the event, that is:

> the probability of getting at least one head in two tossings of the coin
> = the probability of getting head, head (that is, 1/4)
> + the probability of getting head, tail (that is, 1/4)
> + the probability of getting tail, head (that is, 1/4)
> = 1/4 + 1/4 + 1/4
> = 3/4 or 0.75.

So, if we toss a single coin there is the probability of 0.5 that it will come down heads. By doubling our chances, that is, by tossing the coin twice, we increase the probability of achieving one head to 0.75 – doubling the chance only increases the probability by 50%. Can you think of a practical example of this principle? What about having a night watchman whose two states are to be awake or asleep? If we need a watchman awake more than 50% of the time we can achieve the probability of a watchman being awake for 75% of the time if we employ two watchmen each night. (There are undoubtedly better ways of ensuring an awake watchman but we won't go into them just now!) Let's look at a more realistic example. Suppose as a company we have a 50% chance of winning any contract – perhaps we have only one other competitor, which is of similar capability to ourselves. If we tender for two contracts we would have a 75% chance of winning one.

Random Variable

A RANDOM VARIABLE is a numerical description that defines the outcome of an experiment or test. For any experiment, a random variable can be defined such that each possible outcome generates one, and only one, value of the random variable. Examples of random variables are:

Experiment	Random Variable	Possible Values of Random Variables
Test a production run of 100 cars	Number of defective cars found	0, 1, 2, . . . 100
Observe length of a queue	Number of people in the queue	0, 1, 2, etc.
Measure times of a production activity	Length of time taken to carry out production activity	2 mins 50 secs, 3 mins, 4 mins, etc.

A random variable can be described as discrete or continuous depending on the sort of numerical values it takes on. A DISCRETE RANDOM VARIABLE is one that takes on a finite number of values (say, 1 to 5) or an infinite sequence (say 1, 2, 3, etc.). Examples are number of units sold, numbers of customers, etc. A CONTINUOUS RANDOM VARIABLE can take on an infinite number of values in an interval, for example percentages, time, weight, distance. Let's look at a specific example of the continuous random variable of employees' heights. An interval could be defined as all heights between 160 and 200 cms. As an individual's height can theoretically be measured to a very high degree of accuracy, for example, 170.679438 . . . cms, then we can see (we hope) that there is an infinite number of values in this interval.

Probability Distributions

A PROBABILITY DISTRIBUTION for a random variable describes how the probabilities are distributed or spread over the various values that the random variable can assume. Probability distributions provide the bedrock to the theory and understanding of the vitally useful process known as STATISTICAL INFERENCE, and in particular estimation and significance testing. These are covered in the next two chapters.

Let's look at a simple example to help you understand what a probability distribution is. Suppose we are interested in having information on the number of times per month people eat out in a restaurant. Perhaps we are contemplating opening a restaurant in the area and our bank manager wants some evidence on local trade before giving us a bank loan. Let's assume we selected 200 people at random and interviewed them to obtain this data. The results of our survey are set out below:

Table 7.1
Probability Distribution for Eating Out

Random Variable (No. of times eaten out in a restaurant during last month)	Frequency (No. of people who ate out this number of times)	Probability (of people eating out this number of times)
0	20	20/200 = 0.10
1	80	80/200 = 0.40
2	50	50/200 = 0.25
3	40	40/200 = 0.20
4	10	10/200 = 0.05
	200	1.00

The table describes the probability distribution of a discrete random variable – in other words, a DISCRETE PROBABILITY DISTRIBUTION – and it can be shown diagrammatically, as follows:

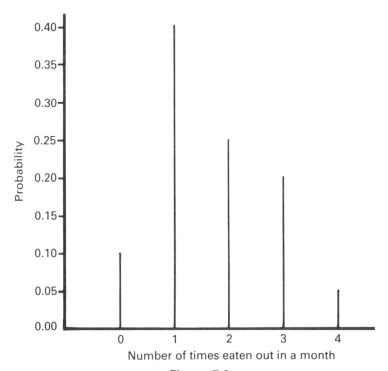

Figure 7.2
*Probability Distribution for
Dining Out in a Restaurant in a Month*

It is quite straightforward to calculate measures of location and dispersion of random variables. It is very similar to the work we did in the last chapter where we were manipulating data. If we take the values of a random variable x as x_1, x_2, x_3 and so on, with the associated probabilities as $p(x_1)$, $p(x_2)$, $p(x_3)$, etc., then

The mean of a random variable x

$$= x_1p(x_1) + x_2p(x_2) \ldots x_np(x_n)$$

$$= \sum_{i=1}^{n} x_ip(x_i)$$

The variance of a random variable x

$$= (x_1 - \text{mean})^2 p(x_1) + (x_2 - \text{mean})^2 p(x_2) \ldots$$
$$(x_n - \text{mean})^2 p(x_n)$$

$$= \sum_{i=1}^{n} (x_i - \text{mean})^2 \, p(x_i)$$

which can be simplified to:

$$\sum_{i=1}^{n} x_i^2 p(x_i) - (\text{mean})^2$$

The standard deviation $= \sqrt{\text{variance}}$

Using our previous example:

Mean value of the random variable (the number of times people eat out each month)

$$= (0 \times 0.1) + (1 \times 0.4) + (2 \times 0.25) + (3 \times 0.2) + (4 \times 0.05)$$
$$= 0.4 + 0.5 + 0.6 + 0.2$$
$$= 1.7$$

In other words, on average people eat out 1.7 times each month. However, eating out is a discrete random variable as we can't actually eat out 0.7 or 1.7 times per month. The people in our sample actually eat out between once and twice per month.

Using our earlier example again and our simplified formula:

The variance of the random variable (the number of times people eat out each month)

$$= (0^2 \times 0.1) + (1^2 \times 0.4) + (2^2 \times 0.25) +$$
$$(3^2 \times 0.2) + (4^2 \times 0.05) - 1.7^2$$

(Take note of where the figures in the above equation have come from. The probabilities p came from Table 7.1 and the mean 1.7 came from the calculation above.)

Continuing with the calculation:

$$\text{Variance} = 0 + 0.4 + 1.0 + 1.8 + 0.8 - 2.89$$
$$= 1.11$$

Standard deviation $= \sqrt{\text{variance}}$

$$= \sqrt{1.11}$$

$$= 1.054$$

Binomial Probability Distribution

A very common and useful type of discrete probability distribution is the BINOMIAL PROBABILITY DISTRIBUTION. An experiment is called BINOMIAL if it has the following characteristics:

a   it consists of a sequence of identical tests;
b   *two* outcomes only are possible on each test, for example, heads or tails, perfect or imperfect;
c   the probability of success (p) stays the same throughout all the trials; so similarly does the probability of failure $(1 - p)$;
d   the trials are independent, that is, the results of one does not affect the results of another. (For example, when a tossed coin comes down heads, there is not a finite supply of heads available, so the next toss of the coin has the same chance of coming down heads as the previous one.)

The random variable we are concerned with here is the number of successes occurring in the trials. The trials could be a series of tosses of a coin or the examination of a number of products for defects – each toss of the coin or each product examined is one trial or test.

For all experiments that can be described in this way (that is, binomial experiments) there is a formula for working out the probability distribution which gives the probability of a certain number of successes in the trials. The formula is:

The probability of x successes in n trials, $p(x)$,

$$= \frac{n!}{x!(n - x)!} p^x (1 - p)^{(n - x)}$$

The exclamation mark (!) or *factorial* is a shorthand used in mathematics to mean:

$$n! = n \times (n - 1) \times (n - 2) \times (n - 3) \ldots 1$$
$$x! = x \times (x - 1) \times (x - 2) \times (x - 3) \ldots 1$$
$$(n - x)! = (n - x) \times (n - x - 1) \times (n - x - 2) \ldots 1$$

Some simple examples are:

$$3! = 3 \times 2 \times 1$$
$$5! = 5 \times 4 \times 3 \times 2 \times 1, \text{ and}$$
$$0! = 1 \text{ (please just accept this)}$$

The formulae for calculating the mean and variance of a random variable with a binomial distribution are quite simple:

$$\text{Mean} = np$$
$$\text{Variance} = np(1 - p)$$

Continuous Probability Distribution

A continuous random variable may assume any value in an interval, for example, weight, distance, time, etc. All of these can take on values of infinite numbers of decimal places, depending on how accurately you wish to measure them. When we talked about a discrete random variable we defined the probability distribution as something which told us the probability of the random variable assuming a particular value. The equivalent expression for a continuous random variable is a PROBABILITY DENSITY FUNCTION for reasons which will become clear later. (See page 92.)

In order to illustrate the concept of a continuous probability distribution, we will use the example of a UNIFORM DISTRIBUTION. Suppose you have a delivery lorry which travels from London to Cardiff. Assume that the journey time can take any value between 150 minutes and 200 minutes. If the probability of a journey time falling in any one-minute interval is the same, that is, it is equally likely to fall between 160 and 161 minutes, and between 174 and 175 minutes, then it is said to have a uniform distribution. Since there are 50 one-minute intervals (between 150 and 200), all of which are equally likely, then the probability of falling in any one-minute interval is 1/50. Now let us look at this distribution in graphical form as we learnt in Chapter 5:

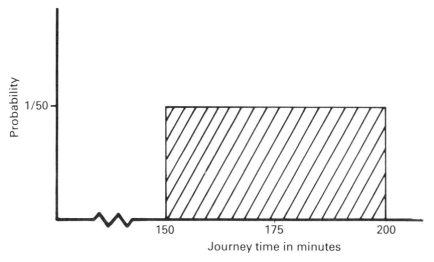

Figure 7.3
Uniform Probability Density Function for Journey Times

What is the probability of the journey time falling between 150 and 175 minutes? Intuitively, since this falls halfway along the total range, we feel that the probability might be 1/2. Alternatively, as budding statisticians we can use the probability formula from page 84:

The probability of an event	= the sum of the probabilities of the constituent events

Probability of a journey time between 150 and 175 minutes, $p(150 - 175)$
= $p(150 - 151) + p(151 - 152)$
  $+ p(152 - 153) . . .$
  $+ p(174 - 175)$
= 25 × 1/50
= 1/2 (just as our intuition suggested)

Another option is to take the area of the graph contained within the intervals 150 and 175.

Here, area = height × width
= 1/50 × 25
= 1/2

Similarly, let's work out the probability of the journey time falling between 160 and 180 minutes. Look at the graph again.

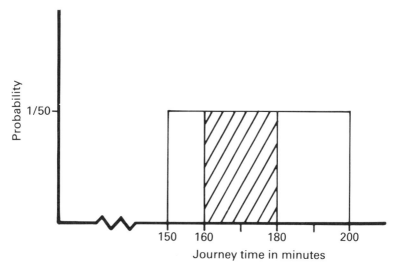

Figure 7.4
Shaded Area Gives the Probability of
Journey Time Falling Between 160 and 180 Minutes

Area = height × width
= 1/50 × 20
= 0.4

Therefore, to find the probability of the journey time falling between 160 and 180 minutes we take the area under the graph bounded by the interval 160 to 180 minutes. Hence we can see that we can calculate the probability of the random variable falling in a particular interval by calculating the area bounded by the distribution curve over that interval. That is why the distribution of a continuous random variable is called a PROBABILITY DENSITY FUNCTION.

We now move on to a slightly more difficult but very important continuous distribution, the normal distribution.

The Normal Distribution

We mentioned the normal distribution in Chapter 5. We said then that statisticians loved the normal distribution because it allowed them to make assumptions about the way data will behave in their calculations. It is almost certainly the most important of the distributions that you will come across. It is vital to the theory of sampling which we cover in the next chapter. Make sure you understand what a normal distribution is, together with its principal characteristics and some of its more important features.

We will not trouble you with the formula that describes the normal curve, the graphical representation of the density function of the normal distribution – it is sufficient for our purposes to know that it is bell-shaped and has the principal features set out in the next paragraph. The curve itself looks like this:

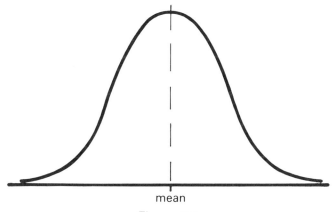

mean

Figure 7.5
A Typical Normal Probability Distribution

The principal features of a NORMAL DISTRIBUTION are as follows:

a   The highest point of the normal curve occurs at the mean. The mean is also the mode and the median for the normal curve (see Chapter 6).

b   The mean of the distribution can be any value, positive, negative or zero.

c   The curve is symmetrical about the mean with tails extending infinitely in both directions and, theoretically, never touching the horizontal (x) axis.

d   The spread of the curve determines the standard deviation, that is, the flatter the curve the larger the standard deviation for the same mean.

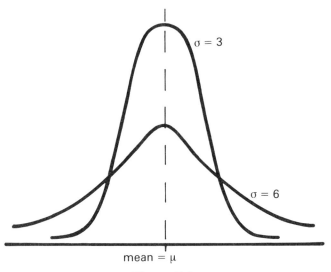

Figure 7.6
Two Normal Distributions with Mean μ,
but Different Standard Deviations

e   The total area under the curve is 1. This is true for all continuous probability distributions.

f   It has the very important feature which applies to all normal distributions, whatever their mean (μ) or standard deviation (σ), that:

68.26% of the time, a normal random variable assumes a

value within plus or minus 1 standard deviation of its mean, that is between $\mu \pm 1\sigma$.

95.44% of the time, a normal random variable assumes a value within plus or minus 2 standard deviations of its mean, that is $\mu \pm 2\sigma$.

99.72% of the time, a normal random variable assumes a value within plus or minus 3 standard deviations of its mean, that is $\mu \pm 3\sigma$.

In other words, the random variable with a normal distribution falls in the interval of $\mu \pm 1\sigma$ for about two-thirds of the time, and nearly all the time in the interval of $\mu \pm 3\sigma$. We will make good use of this feature when we come to sampling in Chapter 8.

You may at some time come across the STANDARD NORMAL DISTRIBUTION. This is a normal distribution with the particular features of a mean of 0 and a standard deviation of 1. In fact *all* normal distributions can be expressed in terms of the standard normal distribution very simply, and special tables have been developed which statisticians find very useful!

Conclusion

We hope that you now understand what a random variable is and that you feel at home with the concept of a probability distribution. We have introduced the fascinating and very important normal distribution. The next two chapters will go on to show how we apply all that we have learned so far to the subjects close to the hearts of all statisticians, sampling and hypothesis testing.

8

Sampling, Estimation and Inference

Introduction

We move on now to talk about the statistical technique, sampling, and the part it can play in providing information for management decision making. You may want to ask 'Why take samples at all?' Well, the purpose of sampling is to produce information about a large population from a small portion of that population – a sample. When the sample is statistically correct we can draw valid conclusions about the larger population by STATISTICAL INFERENCE. Being able to draw these conclusions from a smaller sample than the whole population generally ensures the process will be quicker and less costly than if we were to survey the whole population. By approaching the sampling exercise correctly we will have these early, less costly results without compromising the accuracy too much. However, it is not always necessarily helpful to take a sample. If the population is relatively small in size or the list of the population, the SAMPLING FRAME, is readily accessible (for example, the pay of employees from the payroll file on the computer), it may be easier to work with the population as a whole.

One of the most frequent and well known statistical sampling exercises takes place before elections of political parties in the Western democracies. In Britain we know of the polls that take place before the General Elections which tell us how we are going to vote on the day! Other sampling exercises conducted on a regular basis tell us which of the political parties have the strongest support from the voters and even give us details about the popularity of the various party leaders. Now, the pollsters do not interview the whole population of Great Britain to give us these eye-catching results; they interview a small, statistically valid sample of the population. Most respectable polls give an indication of the size of their sample and sometimes how those people interviewed were selected. The figures can be quite dramatically small. A sample of just over 1,000 people can give a good indication of how the rest of us 26 million voters intend to vote.

Other examples of sampling are:

a   In market research, to find out information, for example, about peoples' attitudes or their purchasing habits.
b   In manufacturing, to test the life of, say, batteries. A sample of 100 would be taken from production and tested to see how long, on average, they last. (This is an example where there is no alternative to sampling – since we do not want to use up all our products in the tests!)
c   In retailing, to try out and test shoppers' reaction to a new product. Suppose we own a chain of 1,000 stores. We may be interested in seeing how well the new product, for example an exotic fruit, will sell. We could try it in a small sample of the stores, say 20. If we tried the product out in all our stores and it failed, we could have the expense and embarrassment of a lot of rotting exotic fruit!

The sample results provide ESTIMATES of what the results might be if the whole population was surveyed. The estimate is unlikely to be exactly the same as the true value for the population as a whole and one of the things we will want to know is how *good* our estimate is, that is, how close it is to the true value for the population.

We will first look at how we choose a sample. We will then go on to discuss *point estimates*. To help us answer the question of how good our estimate is, we need to understand a little about sampling distributions. We will examine in detail the sampling distributions of two important types of estimate – the sample mean and the sample proportion. From these sampling distributions, we will then be able to define confidence limits for these estimates. Finally, we explain how to calculate sample size.

There are several different methods used to select a sample and our choice of method depends on the circumstances, as we will explain later in the chapter. We start with the most common method, simple random sampling, and then go on to discuss systematic sampling, stratified random sampling and cluster sampling.

Simple Random Sampling

We will consider the case where we have a FINITE population, that is, we know the size of the total population. A SIMPLE RANDOM SAMPLE of size *n* from a population size *N* is selected in such a way that every sample of size *n* has the same probability of being selected.

Let us consider a simple case. Suppose we have six cars and want to know with a reasonable degree of accuracy what the petrol consumption figures are. We do not have the resources to monitor all six cars and decide to monitor two of them. How many different pairs of cars (samples) could we pick from the six cars (the population). Let us set out all the possibilities, lettering the cars A to F, inclusive:

AB,   AC,   AD,   AE,   AF
BC,   BD,   BE,   BF
CD,   CE,   CF
DE,   DF
EF

There are 15 different samples we can choose.

You could write each of these 15 samples on a card and put them in a large hat. Pull out a card and, since each card has an equal probability of being picked, that is 1 in 15, then it is a random sample. Now clearly, if our population size was very large, then the number of different samples we could pick would also be very large, and the method we have used above to select the sample would be too laborious. Instead, to help us the statisticians have prepared what are called random number tables, and a section is given in Table 8.1.

Suppose we wanted to pick a sample of 40 cars from a production run of 3,000 cars for testing. We would start by numbering all the cars from 0001 to 3000. Then, using the line in the table marked with a *, we choose numbers in groups of four digits (as there are four digits in the number '3000'): 1058, 1301 (4389 – deleted), 2145, 2134, and so on until we have 40 appropriate numbers, having discarded the numbers with values over 3000.

We can start anywhere in the table and go up, down or across to get our random numbers. The tables are designed in such a way

Table 8.1

Extract from
Random Number Tables

98554	52502	11780	04060	56634	58077	02005	80217	65893	78381
89725	00679	28401	79434	00909	22989	31446	76251	17061	66680
49221	37750	26367	44817	09214	82674	65641	14332	58221	49564
31783	96028	69352	78426	94411	38335	22540	37881	10784	34658
51025	72770	13689	21456	48391	00157	61957	11262	12640	17228
*10581	30143	89214	52134	76280	77823	61674	96898	90487	43998
51753	56087	71524	64913	81706	33984	90919	86969	75553	87375
96050	08123	28557	04240	33606	10776	64239	81900	74880	92654
93998	95705	73353	26933	66089	25177	62387	34932	62021	34044
70974	45757	31830	09589	31037	91886	51780	21912	16444	52881
25833	71286	76375	43640	92551	46510	68950	60168	26399	04599
55060	28982	92650	71622	36740	05869	17828	29377	01020	90851
29436	79967	34383	85646	04715	80695	39283	50543	26875	94047
80180	08706	17875	72123	69723	52846	71310	72507	25702	33449
40842	32742	44671	72953	54811	39495	05023	61569	60805	26580
31481	16208	60372	94367	88977	35393	08681	53325	92547	31622
06045	35097	38319	17264	40640	63022	01496	28439	04197	63858
41446	12336	54072	47198	56085	25215	89943	41153	18496	76869
22301	07404	60943	75921	02932	50090	51949	86415	51919	98125
38199	09042	26771	15881	80204	61281	61610	24501	01935	33256
06273	93282	55034	79777	75241	11762	11274	41685	24117	98311
92201	02587	31599	27987	25678	69736	94487	41653	79550	92949
70782	80894	95413	36338	04237	19954	71137	23584	87069	10407
05245	40934	96832	33415	62058	87179	31542	18174	54711	21882
85607	45719	65640	33241	04852	87636	43840	42242	22092	28975

that there is no bias in the selections, for example, the numbers within the range 2001 to 3000 have no better nor worse chance of being selected than any other range of numbers. We continue until we have 40 numbers within the range 1 to 3000 and, having used the random number tables, we can be confident that the 40 numbers are selected totally randomly. To a certain extent, the advent of computers has overtaken the need for random number tables, as the computer can be programmed to generate random numbers for us.

Systematic Sampling

If there is a very large population from which we are taking our sample it may be too laborious to go through and number the whole population so that we can identify the sample members using random numbers. A much simpler alternative way is to use SYSTEMATIC SAMPLING.

Let us suppose there is a population of 10,000 from which we have decided to take a sample of 500, that is, a ratio of one sample member for every 20 population members. We choose the first sample member randomly from the first 20 members of the population and then take every 20th population member thereafter until we have our sample of 500. This technique is particularly useful if there is an infinite population because, once you have decided upon your sample size, you just keep on going, systematically selecting at your defined interval until you have the sample size you require. The only proviso is that the population must be randomly ordered otherwise a bias could be built into the results.

Stratified Random Sampling

This is a complicated name for quite a simple but very useful concept. With STRATIFIED RANDOM SAMPLING, we divide our population into strata and choose a random sample from each strata. Examples of such strata are geographical location, age groups, factories, etc. This method has the advantage of ensuring that we can obtain information on the stratum, for example a particular age group, as well as enabling us to work out overall estimates for the whole sample.

Cluster Sampling

Getting our data by taking a sample of the population is much cheaper than carrying out a comprehensive survey of the whole population. However, random and even systematic sampling can be very expensive on occasions, so CLUSTER SAMPLING can sometimes be used to reduce sampling costs by concentrating our sampling in a small area. For example, let us say that we are interested in finding out information about the electorate's view on a particular policy which is due to be implemented by the local authority. The voting population could be over 100,000 and we might be seeking a sample of 500. It could be very expensive to go and interview every 2,000th person on the Electoral Register who, probably, would live miles apart. Instead, we could choose a random sample of clusters of voters, perhaps by postal districts, and then the voters within the clusters would form our sample. The best results are obtained when each cluster represents, as closely as possible, a mini version of the whole population. This is important because, if we choose our clusters only from the wealthier parts of the district or vice versa, we could bias the result.

Point Estimates

We explained at the beginning of this chapter that the purpose of sampling is to provide information about a population of interest from a small sample of that population. The types of information about the population that we are interested in might be an average value, a proportion or a standard deviation.

For example, suppose we are interested in the ages of employees who work in a large organization, possibly with a view to providing a new benefits package. It is possible that older employees might be more interested in a good pension package whereas young employees might be more interested in high performance-related payments. Information on the age breakdown of the employees could give management information, not only on the likely attractiveness of different packages, but also on the likely cost, now and over a number of years. We might want to know:

a   the average age of all the employees;
b   the proportion of employees that are, say, under 30 and over 60;
c   the variation in ages of the employees, measured by the standard deviation.

We would choose a sample using one of the methods discussed

earlier in this chapter and then work out from that sample the following statistics:

a   the sample mean;
b   the sample proportions;
c   the sample standard deviation.

These sample statistics will be POINT ESTIMATES of the population statistics, that is of:

a   the population mean;
b   the population proportion;
c   the population standard deviation.

It should be obvious that the information gained from a sample is unlikely to provide an exact estimate of the population statistic of interest and if we were able to choose other samples, we would probably get slightly different results. Let us take a simple example. Suppose the population is our employees and the characteristic of interest is age.

Table 8.2
Population of Ages of Employees

17	42	23	48	29	52	31	59	38	62
63	39	34	57	54	27	23	46	44	19
45	16	22	49	27	54	34	57	62	37
19	45	50	21	27	52	57	34	39	64
62	37	59	33	27	53	47	23	16	43
62	59	54	49	44	19	24	29	34	39
20	45	25	50	30	55	35	60	40	65
26	34	37	42	44	37	33	27	25	28
52	48	47	43	41	40	37	29	29	32
31	34	37	46	44	51	47	33	24	54

We will take two samples of 20 employees using the systematic sampling method. For the first sample we will use as our starting point, say, employee number 4 and for the second sample, employee number 1. We pick every fifth employee for our sample, as follows:

Sample 1		Sample 2	
48	38	17	52
57	44	63	27
49	62	45	54
21	39	19	52
33	16	62	53
49	34	62	19
50	40	20	55
42	25	26	37
43	29	52	40
46	24	31	51

We can now calculate the following:

Population mean = 39.88 years (by adding all the ages in our population and dividing by 100)

Sample mean from sample 1 = 39.45 years (by adding all the ages in our sample and dividing by 20)

Sample mean from sample 2 = 41.85 years (by adding all the ages in our sample and dividing by 20)

As you can see, the sample means give different estimates of the population mean. Usually, of course, we only take one sample and we use it to calculate estimates of the population characteristics of interest to us. Then, what we need to know is how close our estimate is to the population characteristic we are trying to measure. To find this out we must understand a little about sampling distributions.

Sampling Distributions and Confidence Limits

As usual, it is easier to understand a concept by looking at an example. Let us focus our minds on the population which interests us. Suppose we are a mail order firm and we want to know more about our customers so that we can make our advertising more cost-effective. Suppose their income is of particular interest and we want to know:

a   the average income of our customers;
b   the proportion of customers with incomes in excess of £10,000;
c   the range, or variation, in incomes of our customers.

Clearly, our population of interest is *all* our customers who could number 10,000, 100,000 or even more. How would we go about the exercise? The first step would be to choose a sample, of say 100 customers, and obtain data on their incomes. As we have suggested before, we could go on choosing different samples of 100 customers and each time we would get slightly different values for:

a   the sample mean;
b   the sample proportion;
c   the sample standard deviation.

Let us imagine that we carried out the sampling exercise four times, using the same sampling method, and found that the sample mean (in our case, the average income) was as follows:

Table 8.3
*Sample Means from
Sampling Exercise*

Sample Number	Sample Mean (Av. salary)
1	£6,014
2	£6,450
3	£5,995
4	£6,222

If we took 200 of these samples we would find that we could prepare a frequency distribution, as we did in Chapter 4; an example appears in Table 8.4. We could then go on to draw a histogram as we did in Chapter 5 (see Figure 8.1).

This histogram gives the SAMPLING DISTRIBUTION of the sample mean. In other words it describes the way in which the average incomes, calculated from our different samples of 100 customers,

Table 8.4
Frequency Distribution of Sample Means

Mean Income	Frequency	Relative Frequency	
£5,801–5,900	10	.05	(5%)
£5,901–6,000	22	.11	(11%)
£6,001–6,100	38	.19	(19%)
£6,101–6,200	50	.25	(25%)
£6,201–6,300	44	.22	(22%)
£6,301–6,400	24	.12	(12%)
£6,401–6,500	12	.06	(6%)
	200	1.00	(100%)

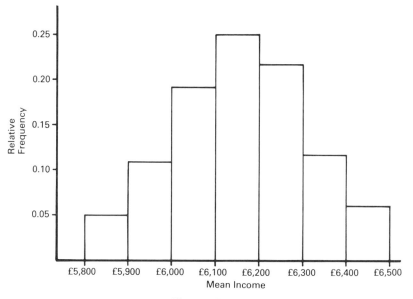

Figure 8.1
Relative Frequency Histogram of Values of Mean Income from 200 Samples

vary due to variations in the different samples. We would get a similar distribution, in shape, if we had worked out a sample proportion. Each, in turn, would be the sampling distribution of that sample statistic.

Let us go back to our example of the average income of our customers. Each time we take another sample we are getting another outcome (do you remember that expression from Chapter 7?) of the sample income. Thus the average income statistic is a random variable (remember that too from Chapter 7) with a distribution and it will be possible to work out the mean and the standard deviation of the sampling distribution of the random variable average income. So, how does this help us to answer the question 'How good is our estimate?'

A very useful and important theorem in statistics is called the CENTRAL LIMIT THEOREM. This tells us that if simple random samples of size n are drawn from a population with mean μ and a standard deviation σ, then the sampling distribution of the sample mean $\bar{x}$ approaches a normal distribution with mean μ and standard deviation $(\sigma/\sqrt{n})$ as the sample size becomes larger. This is important because it means that we can apply the very useful properties of the normal distribution that we discussed in Chapter 7 to the distribution of the sample mean. In practice, *for any sample of 30 or more*, the Central Limit Theorem can apply. If the population distribution itself is known to be normal, then the sampling distribution of the sample mean can also be assumed to be normal for sample sizes below 30.

Now, you will recall from Chapter 7 (pages 94–5) the following very useful characteristics of a normal distribution:

a   68.26% of the time, a normal random variable assumes a value within plus or minus one standard deviation of its mean, that is, 68.26% of the time $\bar{x}$ falls in the range:

$$\mu \pm \frac{\sigma}{\sqrt{n}}$$

b   95.44% of the time, a normal random variable assumes a value within plus or minus two standard deviations of its mean, that is, 95.44% of the time $\bar{x}$ falls in the range:

$$\mu \pm \frac{2\sigma}{\sqrt{n}}$$

c   99.72% of the time, a normal random variable assumes a value within plus or minus three standard deviations of its mean, that is, 99.72% of the time $\bar{x}$ falls in the range:

$$\mu \pm \frac{3\sigma}{\sqrt{n}}$$

Let us look rather closer at case b. This can be expressed a little differently: there is a 95.44% chance or 0.9544 probability that $\bar{x}$ falls in the range $\mu \pm 2\,\sigma/\sqrt{n}$. It is shown by the shaded area in Figure 8.2:

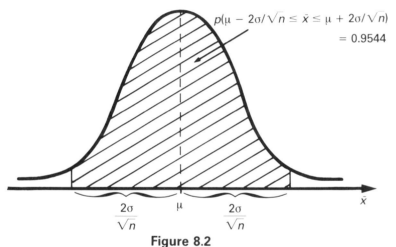

$$p(\mu - 2\sigma/\sqrt{n} \le \bar{x} \le \mu + 2\sigma/\sqrt{n})$$
$$= 0.9544$$

Figure 8.2
Normal Distribution of $\bar{x}$, with Mean μ
and Standard Deviation $\sigma/\sqrt{n}$

However, we might find it more convenient to think in terms of a 95% chance or 0.95 probability of the sample mean $\bar{x}$ falling in a particular interval. It can be shown that:

there is a 95% chance (rather than 95.44%) or a 0.95 probability of the sample mean $\bar{x}$ falling in the range:

$$\mu \pm \frac{1.96\sigma}{\sqrt{n}} \qquad (1.96 \text{ rather than } 2)$$

Similarly:

there is a 99% chance or a 0.99 probability of the sample
mean $\bar{x}$ falling in the range:

$$\mu \pm \frac{2.58\sigma}{\sqrt{n}}$$

In most cases we will not know the population standard deviation
σ and will use our sample standard deviation s to estimate it. (This
may be seen as a bit of a trick, but please accept that it is quite
alright!) Then it can be seen from the above that there is a 95%
chance, or a 0.95 probability that our sample mean $\bar{x}$ will fall in
the range:

$$\mu \pm \frac{1.96s}{\sqrt{n}}$$

Intuitively, we can rewrite this relationship as their being a 95%
chance, or a 0.95 probability, that μ will fall in the range:

$$\bar{x} \pm \frac{1.96s}{\sqrt{n}}$$

(Don't worry if you can't see this. Just accept our word for it.)

These are known as the 95% CONFIDENCE LIMITS for the population mean μ.

Let's look at an example. Suppose we have an organization
which relies heavily on its distribution system. Consider the regular
run between the depot and Outlet A. It is important for scheduling
the vehicles to know the average time taken for this journey and
the range of confidence limits, be they 95%, 99% or whatever.
Assume that we choose a random sample of 30 trips and note the
time taken as set out in the table below:

Table 8.5
Average Journey Times

Number of Minutes Taken on Journey					
160	179	188	180	188	195
185	190	162	165	183	199
167	192	186	181	194	172
182	166	187	172	168	181
175	176	195	161	184	172

The sample mean $\bar{x} = \dfrac{\text{sum of the times}}{30}$

$\qquad\qquad = 179.5$

We are now going to work out the confidence limits. First we work out the sample standard deviation as follows:

Sample variance $s^2 = \dfrac{\Sigma x_i^2 - n\bar{x}^2}{30 - 1}$ (where x_i = the sample points n = the sample size)

$\qquad = \dfrac{160^2 + 179^2 \ldots + 172^2 - 30 \times (179.5)^2}{29}$

$\qquad = \dfrac{970{,}173 - 966{,}608}{29}$

$\qquad = 122.9$

Sample standard deviation $s = \sqrt{122.9}$

$\qquad\qquad\qquad\qquad\quad = 11.1$

Then, we can be 95% confident that the population mean lies within the range:

$$\bar{x} \pm \frac{1.96s}{\sqrt{n}}$$

$$= 179.5 \pm \frac{1.96 \times 11.1}{\sqrt{30}}$$

$$= 179.5 \pm 4.0$$

$$= 175.5 \text{ to } 183.5$$

In other words we can be 95% confident that the average journey time will fall within the range 175.5 to 183.5 minutes.

So now, after all that theory, we begin to see the usefulness of understanding the sampling distribution of the sample mean. It enables us to give, *with confidence*, a range around our estimate within which the population mean will fall.

Similarly we can go through exactly the same process for the population proportion p. The 95% confidence limits for p are:

$$\bar{p} \pm 1.96 \sqrt{\frac{\bar{p}(1 - \bar{p})}{n}}$$

(where $\bar{p}$ is the sample proportion).

Calculating Sample Size

Now that we have some measure of the accuracy of the estimate of our population mean we can go on to look at another very important decision in sampling, the sample size. We can calculate the sample size which is required to give us a certain level of confidence limit. Using the journey times example again, suppose we decided that we wanted to be more precise with our estimate, that is, we wanted to reduce our SAMPLING ERROR. By sampling error, we mean the magnitude of the difference between our estimate and the actual value of the population statistic, in this case the mean.

We calculated with 95% confidence that the population mean lay within plus or minus 4.0 minutes of the sample mean of 179.5. Suppose now we decide that we want to be 95% confident that our population mean lies within a range of plus or minus 3 minutes of the sample mean: giving ourselves a sampling error of 3 minutes. We can calculate the required sample size as follows:

$$3 = \frac{1.96s}{\sqrt{n}} \qquad \text{(see page 108)}$$

We can manipulate our equation to isolate n by multiplying each side by $\sqrt{n}$ and dividing each side by 3, as follow:

$$\sqrt{n} = \frac{1.96s}{3}$$

$$= \frac{1.96 \times 11.1}{3} \quad (s = 11.1 \text{ from page 109})$$

$$= 7.252$$

Therefore $n = 7.252^2 = 52.6$.

Rounding this up, it means that we would need a sample size of 53 trips to be 95% sure of this greater precision that the population mean will fall within plus or minus 3 minutes of the new sample mean.

Conclusion

We hope that you now have a sound understanding of the basic concepts of sampling. Sampling is a vital tool for the gathering of information. It has enormous power, but it must be used with care and understanding. In the next chapter we go on to look at what are called significance and hypothesis tests – they test the significance of our sample results.

9

Hypothesis Testing

Introduction

In the previous chapter we have seen how, by using statistical inference, we can draw conclusions about a population from a sample. We focused our attention on the use of samples for estimating such measures of the population as its mean and proportions of the population possessing a given characteristic. Another major use of sampling is to test hypotheses about the population itself. This technique is frequently adopted in scientific work, for example, testing drugs in pharmaceutical research.

However, hypothesis testing is also of value in the business world, particularly for quality control. Suppose we have a firm making components, in this case, bolts. It is very important that these bolts are of a particular size or very close to it, let us say 3 centimetres in length, or they will be rejected by the customer. Let us use again the Greek letter μ to define the mean or average size for the population of all bolts manufactured.

If $\mu = 3$cm, there is no problem.
If $\mu \neq 3$cm, there is a problem which the firm will have to address.

We tackle this exercise by defining the NULL HYPOTHESIS and the ALTERNATIVE HYPOTHESIS. The null hypothesis (referred to as H_0) is the tentative assumption about the population characteristic that we are going to test. The alternative hypothesis (usually referred to as H_1) covers all other plausible states of the population characteristic. In our example, above:

$$H_0 : \mu = 3$$
$$H_1 : \mu \neq 3$$

The next step is to choose a sample of, say, 50 bolts and measure them. If the sample results are consistent with the null hypothesis, then we are said to ACCEPT H_0. However, if the sample results differ *significantly* from the null hypothesis then we REJECT H_0 and conclude that H_1, the alternative hypothesis, is true. But what do we mean by 'differ significantly'?

First, we need to explain about the different hypothesis tests. There are three types:

a   One type is that already given in the example above where the product either is or is not the correct size, that is, oversized and undersized bolts are both rejected by the customer. It is expressed as follows:

$H_0 : \mu = \mu_T$ where μ is the mean of the population as a whole
$H_1 : \mu \neq \mu_T$ and μ_T is the mean of our test sample.

b   Another type is where the acceptable limit is greater than or equal to a certain specification and the customer would reject an item which was less than the specification. This is expressed as follows:

$$H_0 : \mu \geqslant \mu_T$$
$$H_1 : \mu < \mu_T$$

An example of this type could be a firm making light bulbs which are guaranteed to give 100 hours of life. In order to meet the specification, and not contravene the Trades Descriptions Act, it is important that the light bulbs have an average life of 100 hours or more, that is $\mu \geqslant 100$:

$$H_0 : \mu \geqslant 100$$
$$H_1 : \mu < 100$$

c   The third type is where to meet a specification, some ingredient must not be greater than a certain level. It is expressed as:

$$H_0 : \mu \leqslant \mu_T$$
$$H_1 : \mu > \mu_T$$

An example of this could be in food manufacturing where the level of a certain chemical additive in the product must not be greater than, say, 25 parts per million, that is $\mu \leqslant 25\text{ppm}$:

$$H_0 : \mu \leqslant 25$$
$$H_1 : \mu > 25$$

The first type of test is called a TWO-TAILED TEST and the other two types of test are called ONE-TAILED TESTS. Another set of curious terms you may think, but in fact they refer back to the 'tails' of our old friend the normal distribution. The tails are the sections at either end of the distribution covering those extreme values which are distant from the mean. More of this later because we need to say a few words first about the errors involved in hypothesis testing.

Errors

Now, we would like to think that our test of bolts, light bulbs or whatever would always lead us to accept the null hypothesis, H_0, when it is true and reject it when it is false. However, as we are sure you now appreciate, sampling is not an exact science and there are errors involved. The possible situations that might occur can be shown as follows:

	Accept H_0	Reject H_0
H_0 TRUE	Correct decision	TYPE 1 ERROR
H_0 FALSE	TYPE 2 ERROR	Correct decision

As you will see from this simple table there are two possible types of error:

a   Type 1 error – which occurs when we reject H_0 even when it is true.

b   Type 2 error – which occurs when we accept H_0 even when it is false.

In a sense, hypothesis testing is rather similar to the situation in a criminal court where:

H_0 : the defendant is innocent, and,
H_1 : the defendant is guilty.

The defendant is considered innocent until proven guilty and we are most concerned to ensure that we do not find an innocent person guilty, that is, not to make a Type 1 error. In fact, it is the Type 1 errors that establish the SIGNIFICANCE LEVEL of the test.

Traditionally, and we shall follow this convention in this chapter:

α is defined as the probability of making a Type 1 error;
β is defined as the probability of making a Type 2 error.

Two-tailed Hypothesis Testing

Let us go back to the example of the company manufacturing and testing bolts. Our hypothesis test is expressed as follows:

$$H_0 : \mu = 3$$
$$H_1 : \mu \neq 3$$

We take a sample size of 50 bolts and let us assume the sample average $\bar{x}$ is 2.95 cm and our sample standard deviation s is 0.25 cm. We decide to set our Type 1 error, α, at 0.05, that is, we are content with a 5% chance of accepting H_0 when it is false. As our sample size is over 30 units, by using the Central Limit Theorem (see page 106) we can assume that our sample mean has a normal distribution and test whether this sample mean comes from a population with the characteristic $\mu = 3$.

We want the confidence interval to be such that there is only a 0.05 probability that it will not include the population mean. Look at Figure 9.1:

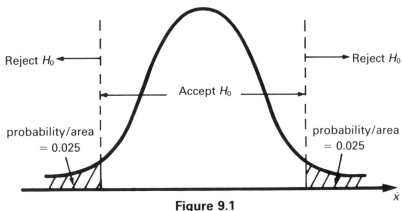

Figure 9.1
Two-tailed Hypothesis Test, with Type 1 error, α = 0.05

We will reject H_0 if μ falls in the shaded areas, that is, in either of the two tails which each have a probability/area of 0.025 and which together give a total Type 1 error of 0.05. Or, we will accept H_0 if μ falls in the range:

$$\bar{x} \pm \frac{1.96s}{\sqrt{n}} \qquad \text{(95\% confidence limits from page 108)}$$

$$= 2.95 \pm \frac{1.96 \times 0.25}{\sqrt{50}}$$

$$= 2.95 \pm \frac{0.49}{7.071}$$

$$= 2.95 \pm 0.07$$

$$= 2.88 \text{ to } 3.02$$

Since the hypothesized population average of 3 cm lies within this interval we accept H_0, that is, we accept the hypothesis. If, on the other hand, the sample average had been 2.9 cm, the confidence interval would have been 2.83 to 2.97 (2.9 ± 0.07) and we would have rejected the null hypothesis as the hypothesized population average of 3 cm is outside this confidence interval of the sample. From the diagram above you will readily see why this is called a two-tailed test!

The same principles apply if we want to carry out a hypothesis test on a population proportion. For example, if we set out the test as follows:

$H_0 : p = p_T$ (where p_T = particular population proportion we
$H_1 : p \neq p_T$ want to test)

then we would accept H_0 at the 95% confidence level, that is
with a Type 1 error of 0.05, if p_T falls in the range:

$$\bar{p} \pm 1.96 \sqrt{\frac{p_T(1 - p_T)}{n}}$$

We have concentrated on the most useful type of hypothesis test,
the two-tailed test. Very similar procedures apply to one-tailed
tests.

Two-population Inference (Independent Samples)

Up until now we have considered only single population situations.
However, in many practical decision-making situations we are
dealing with two different populations – usually because we want
to compare them with each other. For example we might want to
compare the mean salary for female employees with the mean
salary for male employees to test whether or not our equal
opportunity policy is working.

Basically we follow exactly the same procedure as before but
this time we are interested in the difference between the two
sample means. Taking our equal pay example, our hypothesis is
that there is no difference in male/female salaries and can be
expressed as follows:

$H_0 : \mu_1 - \mu_2 = 0$ where μ_1 and μ_2 are the population means of
$H_1 : \mu_1 - \mu_2 \neq 0$ the male and female employees.

This is a two-tailed test.

Let us suppose we carry out our test by randomly sampling the
male and female populations and the results are as follows:

Male Employees	*Female Employees*
$n_1 = 40$	$n_2 = 45$
$\bar{x}_1 = £5,500$	$\bar{x}_2 = £5,300$
$s_1 = £250$	$s_2 = £200$

We will set our probability of a Type 1 error α as 0.01. This means that we are willing to accept a 1% chance of rejecting the null hypothesis even when it is true.

We can show that the 99% confidence interval for $\bar{x}_1 - \bar{x}_2$ is:

$$(\bar{x}_1 - \bar{x}_2) \pm 2.58 \sqrt{\frac{s_1^2}{n_1} + \frac{s_2^2}{n_2}}$$

$$= (5{,}500 - 5{,}300) \pm 2.58 \sqrt{\frac{250^2}{40} + \frac{200^2}{45}}$$

$$= 200 \pm 2.58 \times 49.5$$

$$= 200 \pm 127.7$$

$$= 72.3 \text{ to } 327.7$$

Our null hypothesis, H_0, is $\mu_1 - \mu_2 = 0$. As the value of $\mu_1 - \mu_2$ under our null hypothesis (that is, zero) falls outside the range (72.3 to 327.7) calculated above, we reject the null hypothesis. Given the results of our sample, we cannot be sure that our equal opportunity policy is fully effective. One possible fairer conclusion, as we have only this one sample taken at a single point in time, is that the equal opportunity policy has not yet worked and we still have some way to go.

The pragmatists amongst us might have asked what is the point of all these calculations when we could see from the results of the samples (mean salaries for men and women of £5,500 and £5,300 respectively) that men are better paid than women? What we, as statisticians, are interested in is whether the difference between the two sample means is significant. By *significant* we mean: are the differences between the means likely to represent actual differences in the populations of males and females? Or are they errors induced by the fact that sampling is fraught with uncertainty by its very nature?

Exactly the same procedures can be followed in one-tailed hypothesis tests and where we need to consider proportions rather than means.

We have described how to set up a hypothesis test by defining the null and alternative hypotheses. We discussed the two types of errors we might encounter, but concentrated on the most important error, the Type 1 error, which is the error of rejecting

H_0 when it is true. We have shown how to carry out hypothesis tests using the confidence limit approach and discussed the two different types of test – the two-tailed and one-tailed tests. Finally, we looked at the situation where two populations were involved.

All the hypothesis tests covered so far have involved testing for means and proportions. We are now going to look at two rather different types of hypothesis test.

The Chi-squared Tests for Goodness of Fit and Independence

These hypothesis tests are as straightforward as the ones we have discussed earlier but are used in different situations. We are going to look at two types of test – GOODNESS OF FIT and INDEPENDENCE TESTS – and because they are based on a probability distribution called the Chi-squared (χ^2) distribution, they are called Chi-squared tests.

There are goodness of fit tests for different types of population distributions. However, the most commonly used is the test for what is known as a MULTINOMIAL POPULATION. This is a population where each member of the population is assigned to one, and only one, of several classes or categories. It is just like the binomial except, instead of two outcomes, there can be several outcomes.

Let's look at an example of where you might use a goodness of fit test for a multinomial population. Suppose you are a company which sells cat food. You are about to embark on a major advertising campaign and you will want to know whether it has a significant effect on your market share of cat food sales. Suppose there are three other major brands of cat food product and the market share before your advertising campaign is as follows:

Your Brand	Competitors' Brands		
Paws	Yummy	Furries	Cateats
30%	15%	40%	15%

Following your advertising campaign you carry out a survey of 500 cat owners and ask which cat food they buy. The results are as follows:

Your Brand	Competitors' Brands		
Paws	Yummy	Furries	Cateats
200	50	175	75

Your null hypothesis is that the advertising campaign has had no effect and therefore:

$$H_0 : p_{\text{Paws}} = 0.3, \ p_{\text{Yummy}} = 0.15, \ p_{\text{Furries}} = 0.4, \ p_{\text{Cateats}} = 0.15$$

Your alternative hypothesis is that the population has been affected by the advertising campaign and therefore:

$$H_1 : p_{\text{Paws}} \neq 0.3, \ p_{\text{Yummy}} \neq 0.15, \ p_{\text{Furries}} \neq 0.4, \ p_{\text{Cateats}} \neq 0.15$$

The test looks at differences between the observed results or frequencies from the sample and the expected results or frequencies if the null hypothesis is true. The expected results are arrived at by applying the original market share proportions to the sample of 500 cat owners. This gives the following expected results:

Your Brand	Competitors' Brands		
Paws	Yummy	Furries	Cateats
500×0.3	500×0.15	500×0.4	500×0.15
$= 150$	$= 75$	$= 200$	$= 75$

It is common sense that the bigger the differences between the observed and the expected results, the less likely it is that the null hypothesis is true. The statistic χ^2 is computed using the formula:

$$\chi^2 = \sum_{i=1}^{k} \frac{(o_i - e_i)^2}{e_i}$$

where o_i = observed frequencies for class i
$\quad\quad\ e_i$ = expected frequency for class i
$\quad\quad\ k$ = number of classes

In our example we have four classes (the four brands) and we work out our statistic as follows:

$$\chi^2 = \frac{(200 - 150)^2}{150} + \frac{(50 - 75)^2}{75} + \frac{(175 - 200)^2}{200} + \frac{(75 - 75)^2}{75}$$

$$= \frac{2,500}{150} + \frac{625}{75} + \frac{625}{200} + 0$$

$$= 16.7 + 8.3 + 3.1$$

$$= 28.1$$

If we took lots of samples and calculated their χ^2 values by comparing their observed results with the expected results, the statistic would be shown to have a χ^2 distribution with what is known as $k - 1$ degrees of freedom. In our case $k = 4$, so the number of degrees of freedom is 3. The only requirement is that generally the minimum class size is 5. The chart, shown as Table 9.1, sets out the Chi-squared distribution.

Table 9.1

Chi-squared (χ^2) distribution

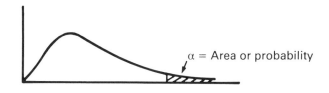

α = Area or probability

d.f. \ α	.250	.100	.050	.025	.010	.005	.001
1	1.32	2.71	3.84	5.02	6.63	7.88	10.8
2	2.77	4.61	5.99	7.38	9.21	10.6	13.8
3	4.11	6.25	7.81	9.35	11.3	12.8	16.3
4	5.39	7.78	9.49	11.1	13.3	14.9	18.5
5	6.63	9.24	11.1	12.8	15.1	16.7	20.5
6	7.84	10.6	12.6	14.4	16.8	18.5	22.5
7	9.04	12.0	14.1	16.0	18.5	20.3	24.3
8	10.2	13.4	15.5	17.5	20.1	22.0	26.1
9	11.4	14.7	16.9	19.0	21.7	23.6	27.9
10	12.5	16.0	18.3	20.5	23.2	25.2	29.6
11	13.7	17.3	19.7	21.9	24.7	26.8	31.3
12	14.8	18.5	21.0	23.3	26.2	28.3	32.9

α d.f.	.250	.100	.050	.025	.010	.005	.001
13	16.0	19.8	22.4	24.7	27.7	29.8	34.5
14	17.1	21.1	23.7	26.1	29.1	31.3	36.1
15	18.2	22.3	25.0	27.5	30.6	32.8	37.7
16	19.4	23.5	26.3	28.8	32.0	34.3	39.3
17	20.5	24.8	27.6	30.2	33.4	35.7	40.8
18	21.6	26.0	28.9	31.5	34.8	37.2	42.3
19	22.7	27.2	30.1	32.9	36.2	38.6	43.8
20	23.8	28.4	31.4	34.2	37.6	40.0	45.3
21	24.9	29.6	32.7	35.5	38.9	41.4	46.8
22	26.0	30.8	33.9	36.8	40.3	42.8	48.3
23	27.1	32.0	35.2	38.1	41.6	44.2	49.7
24	28.2	33.2	36.4	39.4	43.0	45.6	51.2
25	29.3	34.4	37.7	40.6	44.3	46.9	52.6
26	30.4	35.6	38.9	41.9	45.6	48.3	54.1
27	31.5	36.7	40.1	43.2	47.0	49.6	55.5
28	32.6	37.9	41.3	44.5	48.3	51.0	56.9
29	33.7	39.1	42.6	45.7	49.6	52.3	58.3
30	34.8	40.3	43.8	47.0	50.9	53.7	59.7
40	45.6	51.8	55.8	59.3	63.7	66.8	73.4
50	56.3	63.2	67.5	71.4	76.2	79.5	86.7
60	67.0	74.4	79.1	83.3	88.4	92.0	99.6
70	77.6	85.5	90.5	95.0	100.0	104.0	112.0
80	88.1	96.6	102.0	107.0	112.0	116.0	125.0
90	98.6	108.0	113.0	118.0	124.0	128.0	137.0
100	109.0	118.0	124.0	130.0	136.0	140.0	149.0

The χ^2 distribution is a family of distributions where each is distinguished by a single parameter, its *degree(s) of freedom*. Entries in the table give χ^2_α values, where α is the type 1 error or the area/probability in the upper tail of the χ^2 distribution. For example, for $\alpha = .050$ and with 8 degrees of freedom $\chi^2_{0.05} = 15.5$.

Let's see how we use the table. First we must choose our significance level (Type 1 error): let's choose $\alpha = 0.05$. We reject the null hypothesis if the differences between observed and expected frequencies are large, that is, when χ^2 is large. Therefore our rejection area of 0.05 is the upper tail of the distribution. In this case there are four classes ($k = 4$) and therefore there are 3 degrees of freedom. From the table we look across row 3 and down column 0.050 and we find:

$$\chi^2_{0.05} = 7.81$$

As our value of χ^2, 28.1, is greater than the value of 7.81 from the table it falls in the shaded area of the χ^2 distribution shown in Table 9.1 and therefore we reject the null hypothesis. This tells us that the market share structure has changed but not how or why. However, from observation of the results, it can be seen that Paws has gained at the expense of Yummies and Furries, with Cateats share being unaffected. Therefore it would not be unreasonable to conclude that the advertising campaign has been a success. 'Well,' says the cynic, 'we could have told you that, by simple observation of the sample results.' 'Possibly,' says the Statistician, 'but you do not know whether the differences observed in the sample results are merely due to chance. Our test has enabled us to say that the result is significant at the 5% level.' Hence these tests are often called significance tests. You can see too where the term *goodness of fit* comes from – because what we are testing is whether our observed (from the sample) results are a good fit with the results we would expect if our null hypothesis is true.

We will now go on to look at another application of the χ^2 test, the test of independence.

Test of Independence

As the name indicates, a test of independence is a test for the independence of two variables. For example you might want to see whether salary or progress in a company was independent of the sex of the employees. You might wish to examine whether consumer preference for, say, cigarettes was independent of age or whether production was independent of the day of the week, etc. Let us take a very simple example. Suppose you wanted to determine whether or not there were differences in preference for full cream milk, semi-skimmed milk and skimmed milk between the different age groups. Let us assume we are interested in the under 25s, and the 25 and over age groups only.

Our hypotheses are as follows:

H_0 : milk preference is independent of whether the milk consumer is under 25 or 25 and over.

H_1 : milk preference is not independent of whether the milk consumer is under 25 or 25 and over.

Our next step is to carry out a survey of, say, 300 milk drinkers. Let us suppose the results are as follows:

Consumer	Full Cream	Semi-Skimmed	Skimmed	Total
Under 25	20	30	50	100
25 and over	50	80	70	200
Total	70	110	120	300

(A table such as the above which sets out all possible combinations of available contingencies is called a CONTINGENCY TABLE.)

These are our observed results. Just as in the test of goodness of fit, we next need to work out the expected results if the null hypothesis is true. If there are no preference differences between the two age groups, then we could work out the expected proportions from the total results as follows:

proportion preference for full cream   = 70/300 = 0.23
proportion preference for semi-skimmed = 110/300 = 0.37
proportion preference for skimmed   = 120/300 = 0.40

If we then apply these proportions to the totals for each age group, we arrive at the following expected frequencies:

Consumer	Full Cream	Semi-Skimmed	Skimmed	Total
Under 25	23	37	40	100
25 and over	46	74	80	200
Total	69*	111*	120	300

*due to rounding errors

It is helpful for the arithmetic to combine the observed results and the expected results into one table, as follows:

Consumer	Full Cream	Semi-Skimmed	Skimmed
Under 25	20/23	30/37	50/40
25 and over	50/46	80/74	70/80

We then compute a similar statistic as before using the formula:

$$\chi^2 = \sum_i \sum_j \frac{(o_{ij} - e_{ij})^2}{e_{ij}}$$

where o_{ij} = observed result in the contingency table for row i and column j

e_{ij} = expected result in the contingency table for row i and column j

This looks very complicated but all it means is that we are working out our formula

$$\frac{(\text{observed} - \text{expected})^2}{\text{expected}}$$

and summing over all our classes or entries in the table. From our example:

$$\chi^2 = \frac{(20 - 23)^2}{23} + \frac{(30 - 37)^2}{37} + \frac{(50 - 40)^2}{40} + \frac{(50 - 46)^2}{46}$$

$$+ \frac{(80 - 74)^2}{74} + \frac{(70 - 80)^2}{80}$$

$$= \frac{9}{23} + \frac{49}{37} + \frac{100}{40} + \frac{16}{46} + \frac{36}{74} + \frac{100}{80}$$

$$= 6.30$$

This statistic again can be shown to have the χ^2 distribution. The number of degrees of freedom are worked out as follows:

$$(\text{number of rows} - 1) \times (\text{number of columns} - 1)$$

In our case:

$$1 \times 2 = 2$$

Let us now test for independence at the 5% significance level. As before, we will reject the null hypothesis for large values of χ^2. From the table, looking along row 2 and down column 0.050:

$$\chi^2_{0.05} = 5.99$$

As our computed χ^2, 6.30, is greater than 5.99 we reject the null hypothesis and conclude that the preference for different types of milk is not independent of whether the consumer is under 25 years of age or 25 years and over. Again, strictly speaking, we can draw no further conclusion about the possible relationship. However, observation of the contingency table shows us that the older age group appears to have a preference for the full cream and semi-skimmed milk, whereas the younger age group has a preference for skimmed milk.

This procedure has, again, proved to be another simple but useful test. The only rules we have to remember are that the observed results are always expressed in whole numbers – they are frequencies of occurrence – and that each class (for example under 25, 25 and over) size should generally be greater than 5. If we are dealing with a large number of classes and we are close to this minimum class size, then we may choose to combine, or group, some of the classes. Also, we must remember that the test only tells us about whether there is independence or not between classes. It cannot and does not tell us anything about the nature or causes of the relationship. However, it is usually quite easy to deduce some simple conclusions about the relationship by observation of the contingency table.

Conclusion

Well, we have covered a range of hypothesis and significance tests to suit quite a wide variety of situations. Although they sound rather daunting at first, we hope we have shown that once you understand the principles, they are in fact very easy and straightforward to carry out.

10

Regression and Correlation

Introduction

As a manager you may often find yourself faced with drawing conclusions or making recommendations based on the relationship between different variables. For example, as a Personnel Manager you may be interested in looking at whether absenteeism is related to some factor such as age, hours worked, distance from home to work, etc. As a Marketing Manager, you may be interested to see if sales are related to the amount of money spent on advertising, and so on. Regression analysis and correlation are techniques which can help us all in this area of decision making.

Regression Analysis

REGRESSION ANALYSIS is a technique which enables us to describe the relationship between variables using a mathematical equation. In regression analysis there are two types of variable, described as DEPENDENT and INDEPENDENT:

a   *The Dependent Variable.* The dependent variable is the variable being predicted by the relationship; in the above examples, absenteeism and sales would be dependent variables.
b   *The Independent Variable.* The independent variable is the variable which is being used to predict the dependent variable. Again, for example, age, hours worked and distance from home to work would be independent variables used to predict absenteeism in Personnel, and money spent on advertising would be an independent variable used to predict sales.

In this first section we are going to look at the simplest form of regression analysis, SIMPLE LINEAR REGRESSION. This is used in situations where there are only two variables – one independent and one dependent variable – and the relationship between them can be described as a straight line. Situations involving two or more independent variables are analysed by using multiple regression techniques and these will be described briefly in the third section. In the second section we will look at correlation. Whereas in linear regression we are interested in finding a mathematical equation relating two variables, with correlation we are interested in determining the extent to which the variables are related, or the strength of the relationship.

Linear Regression

Let us take our usual simple example. Suppose you are a haulier. Up until now, for each tender you have submitted you have prepared detailed figures on the cost of the work. You are now expanding and you want a simple way to work out a cost for a job. You suspect that the most important influence on the cost of the job is the distance to be travelled. You want to test whether or not this is the case and so look back at the last eight jobs and obtain the data on them which can be summarized as follows:

Table 10.1

Comparison of Haulage Cost against Distance

Job	Distance (Miles)	Cost (£)
1	20	200
2	25	250
3	35	275
4	37	300
5	48	400
6	60	450
7	75	500
8	80	600

The first step is to present the information graphically, by plotting the jobs on a graph of cost against distance. Traditionally, as we are trying to predict cost, that is, the dependent variable, we put cost on the vertical axis (the y axis) and the independent variable, distance, on the horizontal axis (the x axis). The subsequent graph, shown below, is known as a SCATTER DIAGRAM:

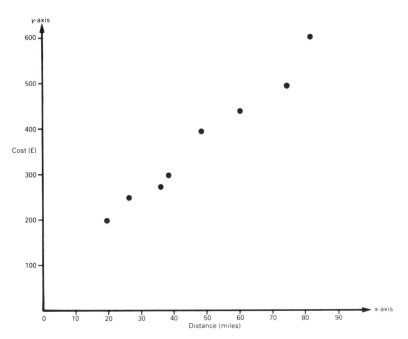

Figure 10.1
Scatter Diagram of Cost/Job against Distance Travelled

The scatter diagram shows us that there does appear to be a linear relationship. A graph showing a straight line or linear relationship between two sets of data can be expressed in the form of a mathematical equation

$$y = a + bx$$

where:

a is the intercept where the graph intersects the y axis (that is, the value of y when $x = 0$)

b is the slope of the line (the bigger the value of b the greater the slope, i.e., the greater the increase in y for a unit increase in x; b can be negative which means that y decreases as x increases).

What we need to do is find the straight line which best fits the points in the scatter diagram. Suppose we define the best fit for the line as:

$y = a_o + b_o x$ (where a_o and b_o are the values of a and b associated with the specific straight line)

then for value of $x = x_i$, the predicted value of y_i would be $a_o + b_o x_i$.

We define the PREDICTION ERROR as:

actual value − predicted value

$$y_i - (a + b_o x_i)$$

We define our line of best fit as one for which:

a   the sum of errors is zero (that is the sum of the differences of the points above and below our line), the positive and negative errors, cancel out.

b   the sum of these errors squared is minimized. The errors are squared to remove the effect of the positive and negative signs.

This is known as the LEAST SQUARES METHOD and it can be shown that the best fit line, $y = a_0 + b_0 x$, is when:

$$a_0 = \frac{\Sigma y}{n} - b_0 \frac{\Sigma x}{n}$$

$$b_0 = \frac{\Sigma xy - \dfrac{\Sigma x \, \Sigma y}{n}}{\Sigma x^2 - \dfrac{(\Sigma x)^2}{n}}$$

where n is the number of observations or points on the scatter diagram.

Going back to our example, it is helpful to set out a table with the following computations:

Table 10.2

Comparison of Haulage Cost against Distance – Useful Tabulations

Job	Distance	Cost		Distance Squared	Cost Squared
	x	y	xy	x^2	y^2
1	20	200	4,000	400	40,000
2	25	250	6,250	625	62,500
3	35	275	9,625	1,225	75,625
4	37	300	11,100	1,369	90,000
5	48	400	19,200	2,304	160,000
6	60	450	27,000	3,600	202,500
7	75	500	37,500	5,625	250,000
8	80	600	48,000	6,400	360,000
	380	2,975	162,675	21,548	1,240,625
	Σx	Σy	Σxy	Σx^2	Σy^2

NB. The y column is not required to calculate the regression line, but is included above as it will be used in a future calculation (see page 134).

Substituting the values from the table into the formulae on page 130 we get:

$$b = \frac{\Sigma xy - \dfrac{\Sigma x \Sigma y}{n}}{\Sigma x^2 - \dfrac{(\Sigma x)^2}{n}}$$

$$= \frac{162,675 - \dfrac{380 \times 2,975}{8}}{21,548 - \dfrac{380 \times 380}{8}}$$

$$= \frac{21,362.5}{3,498}$$

$$= 6.1$$

$$a = \frac{\Sigma y}{n} - b\frac{\Sigma x}{n}$$

$$= \frac{2,975}{8} - 6.1 \times \frac{380}{8}$$

$$= 371.9 - 289.8$$

$$= 82.1$$

Therefore our estimated regression equation is:

$$y = 82.1 + 6.1x$$

This shows that there is a positive intercept on the y axis (at £82.1) and that the slope is such that cost increases with distance at a rate of 6.1:1. Figure 10.2 shows our regression line:

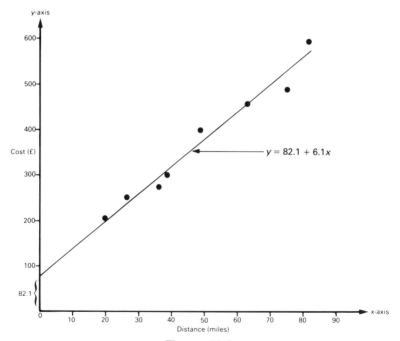

Figure 10.2
Estimated Regression Line

How would we use this equation? Suppose we want to tender for a job with a distance of 40 miles, what would be the cost? Using our regression equation we get:

$$y = 82.1 + 6.1x$$
$$= 82.1 + 6.1 \times 40$$
$$= 82.1 + 244$$
$$= 326.1$$

That is, the cost for a journey of 40 miles would be £326.10.

However, we might also want to get some idea of how good a *fit* our regression line is to the raw data. The measure used is called the COEFFICIENT OF DETERMINATION and is usually denoted by the symbol r^2. It shows how much of the error has been reduced by finding the regression line. The coefficient of determination is, in fact, the proportion of the total sum of squares (without using regression) that can be explained using the estimated regression equation, that is:

$$r^2 = \frac{\text{Sum of squares explained by regression}}{\text{Total sum of squares (before regression)}}$$

The coefficient of determination can be computed by using the following formulae:

Sum of squares explained by regression =

$$\frac{\left(\Sigma xy - \dfrac{\Sigma x\, \Sigma y}{n} \right)^2}{\Sigma x^2 - \dfrac{(\Sigma x)^2}{n}}$$

Total sum of squares before regression =

$$\Sigma y^2 - \frac{(\Sigma y)^2}{n}$$

Taking these formulae into our example we have:

Sum of squares explained by regression

$$= \frac{\left(162{,}675 - \dfrac{380 \times 2{,}975}{8}\right)^2}{21{,}548 - \dfrac{380 \times 380}{8}}$$

$$= \frac{(162{,}675 - 141{,}312.5)^2}{21{,}548 - 18{,}050}$$

$$= \frac{456{,}356{,}406.2}{3{,}498}$$

$$= 130{,}462.1$$

Total sum of squares before regression

$$= 1{,}240{,}625 - \frac{2{,}975 \times 2{,}975}{8}$$

$$= 1{,}240{,}625 - 1{,}106{,}328.1$$

$$= 134{,}296.9$$

Therefore $r^2 = \dfrac{130{,}462.1}{134{,}296.9} = 0.971$

Our estimated regression equation has accounted for 0.971 or 97.1% of the total sum of squares. We would be delighted with a result as high as this in practice, as the closer r^2 is to 1 (or in explaining 100% of the total sum of squares) the better is the fit of our regression line.

The arithmetic gets somewhat tedious for situations with lots of observations. However, there are lots of computer packages on the market these days that work it all out for you.

Correlation

There may be decision-making situations where we are not interested in finding a linear equation relating two variables but instead want to know the extent to which two variables are related. We use the statistic, the CORRELATION COEFFICIENT, to establish the strength of the relationship between two variables. The features of the correlation coefficient are:

a   The value lies between -1 and $+1$.

b   A value of $+1$ means that the two variables are perfectly related in a positive sense, that is, as one increases so does the other. Positive values close to $+1$ show a strong positive relationship – see the scatter diagram in Figure 10.3a.

c   A value of -1 means that the two variables are perfectly related in a negative sense, that is, as one increases the other one decreases. Negative values close to -1 show a strong negative relationship – see the scatter diagram in Figure 10.3b.

d   Values close to 0 show that there is no *linear* relationship – see the scatter diagram in Figure 10.3c.

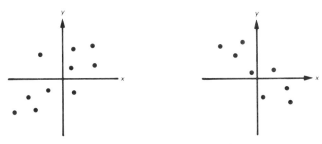

Figure 10.3a
Scatter Diagram
– x and y Positively Related

Figure 10.3b
Scatter Diagram
– x and y Negatively Related

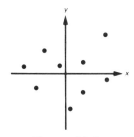

Figure 10.3c
Scatter Diagram – x and y are Not Linearly Related

The correlation coefficient, usually denoted by r, is defined by:

$$r = \pm \sqrt{\text{coefficient of determination}}$$

or, from page 133

$$r = \frac{\Sigma xy - \dfrac{\Sigma x \, \Sigma y}{n}}{\sqrt{\left[\Sigma x^2 - \dfrac{(\Sigma x)^2}{n}\right] \times \left[\Sigma y^2 - \dfrac{(\Sigma y)^2}{n}\right]}}$$

In our example on page 134, $r^2 = 0.971$, therefore

$r = \pm \sqrt{0.971}$

   $= \pm 0.985$, showing a strong positive correlation between distance in miles and cost in pounds.

There are some very important points that need to be borne in mind when using correlation analysis. In fact caution is the order of the day in interpreting our results. We have to be aware that the result on its own tells us little or nothing about the meaning or implications of the relationship other than whether it is strong or not. To explain this point we can use the example of the relationship between cigarette smoking and lung cancer. Originally, the *statistical* evidence was available before the *medical* evidence. The high correlation *suggested* that there was a link between the two but the physical evidence was not available, and until the scientists identified the physical link, the statistical relationship could not be confirmed.

The reason for caution is that it is quite easy to find examples where two variables are correlated but where it is obvious that changes in the one are not caused by changes in the other. Let us take three kinds of examples:

a Each variable may be quite independently related to another third variable, for example, there can be quite a high correlation between the price of washing machines and the price of cars – merely because both are related to a third variable, time.

b The variables may be related via another, intermediate variable. For example, you might find that propensity to have car accidents decreases with the age of the driver. It clearly does not make sense that mere increase in age is reducing the incidence of car accidents – the reason is probably that with increasing age comes increasing caution and there is no causal relationship between the two variables.

c The variables might be linked by sheer chance, sometimes called a nonsense correlation. For example, in the 1930s a *statistical* link was noted between the number of radios in use and the number of suicides. It is possible to test for this chance relationship but we shall not cover it in this book. Readers should simply be aware that the possibility exists.

The final point to be borne in mind is that this chapter has been about testing for a *linear*, that is a straight line, relationship. The two variables could be related in other ways that we will not be covering. Examples of non-linear relationships are curvilinear and exponential, as shown in Figures 10.4a and 10.4b.

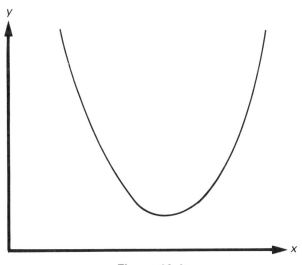

Figure 10.4a
A Curvilinear Relationship

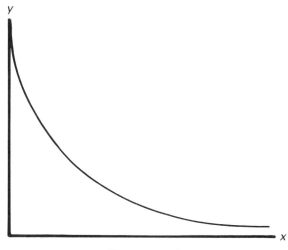

Figure 10.4b
An Exponential Relationship

Multiple Regression

MULTIPLE REGRESSION sounds a rather grand term for what is really a very simple extension of linear regression. Instead of having only one independent variable, we have two or more. In the real world of business this is very useful as, by and large, business situations are complex and there may be a number of factors underlying a particular result. For example, if we are launching a new product we might well advertise in newspapers, on television, local radio, etc., and wish to know the impact of each of these forms of advertising on the sales results. Alternatively, we might need to understand what led to a good performance in our sales force – considering factors such as age, years of experience, training, sex, etc.

We do not intend to explain how to carry out a multiple regression in this book, but to tell you enough to recognize when it would be helpful to use this technique and to appraise you of some of its difficulties. There are several computer packages available which will do all the hard work of the calculations – you just need to be aware when the technique might be useful.

First, we must explain the basic concept. Suppose you are trying to examine a particular variable, for example the sales of a new product, and you suspect it is dependent on a number of other variables, x_1, x_2, x_3, etc. In our example above, the variables would be the different types of advertising. To start, we set up our equation similarly to the way we did in the linear case:

$$y = a + b_1 x_1 + b_2 x_2 + b_3 x_3 + b_4 x_4 \ldots + b_n x_n$$

where y is the dependent variable and $x_1, x_2 \ldots x_n$ are the independent variables.

Now, from this base we can carry out all sorts of interesting tasks:

a We can calculate the values of b_1 to b_n and hence use our equation to predict values of y from different values of x_1 to x_n. As with the linear situation, we can only be confident about such predictions within the range x_1 to x_n.

b We can find out how good a fit the equation is to our data using r^2, the coefficient of determination.

c We can test whether there is a significant relationship between the dependent variable and independent variables. We can do this as a total and also test each independent variable. Now often, our so-called independent variables are not independent. For example, in our sales force performance, age and years of experience might be related. We might find that years of experience is not a significant factor when we have age in the equation, although it might be if age was not considered, since age proved to be the more powerful influence. In this case we would not bother with years of experience in our equation. As far as is possible, it is best to avoid including variables that are highly correlated as it is difficult to separate out the effect of the individual independent variables on the dependent variable.

d We can calculate the importance of each independent variable in explaining the differences in the dependent variables.

It is important to remember again that this technique is based on *linear* relationships. There are lots of other relationships, for example, those that are curvilinear, but the mathematics becomes a bit more tricky, so they are not tackled here.

Conclusion

Well, we hope that wasn't too bad! Regression and correlation techniques are simple but very powerful statistical tools. However, as we have tried to point out, the user must beware of trying to draw too many conclusions. We set off with simple linear regression and correlation which are both quite easy to understand, but in practice, it is multiple regression which enables us to cope with more complex situations and which will prove most useful in the business world.

11

Forecasting and Time Series

Introduction

This chapter looks at the very useful technique of forecasting; useful in the sense that it can help managers from all professions to focus on what is likely to happen in the future. To be able to predict the future accurately is to be rich beyond comparison and if that were capable of being achieved we would need no other business skills at all and most of us would be redundant!

For any organization, whatever its size, it is vital to plan ahead. Depending on the size and nature of the business, a manager may be required to plan a year ahead or perhaps even twenty years ahead. If you are a manager in a manufacturing business you will need to forecast production levels in order to plan for your raw materials, schedule production lines and assess your labour requirements, etc. If you are in retail you will need quite detailed sales forecasts in order to prepare your buying plans, assess your inventory levels, etc. Many large scale businesses will plan at least five years ahead and sometimes more in order to forecast their requirements for new factories, shops or warehouses and hence their requirements for capital investment.

This chapter, then, explains the techniques, but we must remember that our results can be only as good as the data we use in the predictions and the extent to which the future will continue along the same lines as the past. Our fallibility in this respect leaves a place for the business professional and manager to exercise his/her judgement in pursuit of business objectives.

As you will readily appreciate, managers could spend a lot of time trying to forecast the future. How is it done? Do they use a crystal ball – or, its modern equivalent, the computer? In fact, there are various ways to approach the problem of forecasting and these fall into two main types:

a   quantitative methods, and
b   qualitative methods.

Quantitative methods use statistical techniques to analyse the historical data in order to predict the future. If we use only historical data relating to the particular item we are trying to forecast, then the forecasting technique is called a TIME SERIES method. For example, if we are a retailer of prams and are trying to forecast sales of prams, then a time series approach would analyse the historical data on pram sales. If, however, we are going to use historical data relating to other variables, then we use what is called a CAUSAL APPROACH. In a causal approach to forecasting pram sales we might decide to look at the pattern of births to predict our pram sales. We would use linear or multiple regression techniques to help us. In this chapter we are going to concentrate on the time series method.

Qualitative methods usually involve using the judgements of experts as to what the future will hold for us. This is a particularly useful approach if there is no historical data, for example, on the launch of a new product. It is also useful if it is known that something has happened to render the historical data a poor guide to the future. Examples could be where there has been an advance in technology and the cost of the product drops dramatically, or where the government suddenly reduces the rate of VAT on the product putting it within the purchasing range of a much wider market. One particular qualitative method used is the DELPHI APPROACH, which was developed by the Rand Corporation. With this method a panel of experts are each asked to fill in a questionnaire giving their view of the future for, say, a product sales. From the results of the first questionnaire a second is produced which includes the range of opinions of the group. Members of the panel are asked to reconsider their views in the light of the new information from the group. The process goes on until a measure of consensus is reached. The Delphi approach is a fairly sophisticated technique and it is likely that in many businesses the qualitative method will simply involve a group of managers sitting around a table thrashing out what appears to be the best forecast for the future.

Other qualitative methods often used, particularly for short term forecasting, are called BOTTOM UP and TOP DOWN forecasting. In the *bottom up* approach, managers at the lowest level are asked to make a judgement on what, for example, their sales are going to be and then these forecasts are compiled together. Let us consider the situation in a large retail chain of several stores, with each store consisting of many departments. In the first instance all the department managers in all the stores would be asked to estimate their sales increase for the next year, based on their local knowledge. These departmental estimates would be combined to give the forecast increase for each store and, when the store increases are combined, this produces the forecast increase in sales for the whole chain. Top management would then consider the overall result in the light of their knowledge of the wider environment, such as the economic situation, and might accept the overall forecast or vary it according to their assessment.

The *top down* approach works in the reverse order. Top management will lay down their view of the likely increase in sales. This sales forecast will then be allocated across individual stores and the head of each store will allocate the forecast increase across departments.

There are advantages and disadvantages to both approaches. *Bottom up* is useful where local conditions can have a significant effect. For example, the sales increase for a store in a rapidly expanding new town is likely to be considerably greater than that for a store in an established area. Also, the approach is thought to be more motivational because those who have to achieve the target forecast have actually been involved in the decision making for the forecast. The *top down* approach is useful where there are few local variations and the expertise to make the forecasts is concentrated in the head office.

Although the qualitative approach is widely used, we believe that, where it is appropriate and possible to use it, the quantitative approach can produce better results. Because of this we are going to concentrate on the quantitative methods in this chapter and, in particular, the time series approach.

Structure of a Time Series

A time series is simply a set of results for a particular variable of interest, for example, sales, births, etc., taken over a period of time. In order to try and understand the pattern in a time series of data it is helpful to consider what is known as the structure of the time series. There are four separate elements to consider:

- trend
- cyclical
- seasonal
- irregular.

Trend Element

In a set of time series data, the measurements are taken at regular intervals, possibly hourly, daily, weekly, monthly, quarterly, yearly, etc. There will almost certainly be random fluctuations in the data but in some cases the data will also exhibit a shift either to lower or higher values over the time period in question. This movement is called the TREND in the time series and is usually the result of some long term factors such as changes in consumer expenditure, changes in technology, demographic trends, etc.

There may be various trend patterns. Set out in Figures 11.1a to 11.1d are some examples comparing sales over time. In our time series graphs, time is always along the x axis and the variable being measured along the y axis. Suppose these are sales of consumer durables. Figure 11.1a shows that sales are increasing steadily over time and could represent dishwashers where the market is steadily expanding. Figure 11.1b shows that sales are decreasing steadily over time. Perhaps this could represent the sales of black and white televisions where the market has been overtaken by colour TVs. Figure 11.1c shows a very interesting pattern, a non-linear trend, where sales set off slowly then show a period of rapid growth and finally level off. Students of marketing will recognize this graph as the very common product life cycle, where sales of the product are measured from the date of product launch, through its growth period until saturation point is reached and its sales remain steady. Figure 11.1d shows no trend in sales over time – neither increases nor decreases. This could represent the sales of a basic commodity such as potatoes where, with no change in the size of the population, sales might remain quite steady over a long period of time. There may be an occasional

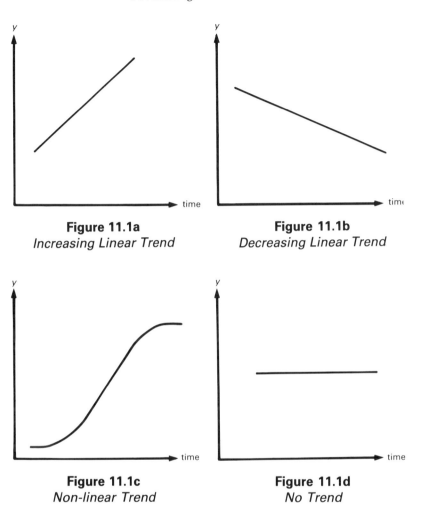

Figure 11.1a
Increasing Linear Trend

Figure 11.1b
Decreasing Linear Trend

Figure 11.1c
Non-linear Trend

Figure 11.1d
No Trend

blip due to, say, a health scare or, alternatively, the promotion of high fibre jacket potatoes, but overall there is a steady pattern.

Cyclical Element

We may have a time series which displays a trend of some sort but in addition shows a cyclical pattern of alternate sequences of observation above and below the trend line. Any regular pattern of observations of this type which lasts longer than a year is called the CYCLICAL ELEMENT of the time series. The graph in Figure 11.2, below, displays a cyclical pattern of sales. This is, in fact, a very common occurrence, representing cyclical fluctuations in the economy as evidenced, for example, by retail sales.

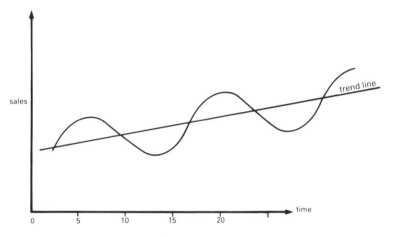

Figure 11.2
Cyclical Fluctuations

Seasonal Element

Whereas the cyclical pattern is displayed over a number of years, there may be a pattern of variability within one year periods. For example, the sales of lawn mowers are likely to peak in the second or third quarters of the year, whereas the sales of toys will peak in the pre-Christmas period. The element of the time series which represents variability due to seasonal influences is called, not surprisingly, the SEASONAL ELEMENT. However, while it normally refers to movements over a one-year period, it can also refer to any repeating pattern of less than one year's duration. For example, daily passenger figures on the London Underground will show clear seasonal movements within the day, with peaks around the rush hour periods of 7.30am to 9.00am and 4.30pm to 6.30pm, moderate levels during the remainder of the day and a tailing off in travel during the evening.

Irregular Element

Finally we come to the IRREGULAR ELEMENT which is that element which cannot be explained by the trend, the cyclical and/or the seasonal elements. It represents the random variability in the time series caused by unanticipated and non-recurring factors which, by their very nature, are unpredictable.

So let's recap briefly. A time series can show a trend (a long term shift in the data), a cyclical pattern (where the measurements show alternate sequences above and below the trend line over periods greater than a year), a seasonal pattern of movements within a year and, finally, an irregular element which is the random variability in the data.

In the following section we will look at forecasting techniques which are appropriate for fairly stable time series, where there are no significant trends, cyclical or seasonal patterns. These are the smoothing methods. We will then go on to look at how to forecast from a time series with a long-term linear trend and finally how to deal with seasonal elements.

Smoothing Methods

SMOOTHING METHODS are used to smooth out the irregular element of time series where there are no significant trends, cyclical or seasonal patterns. There are two commonly used smoothing methods:

a   moving average, and
b   exponential smoothing.

We shall discuss only the moving average method in detail as, by and large, it meets most needs. Exponential smoothing is an alternative method, which is a little more complex to calculate, but has the advantage that it requires very little historical data to put it into use. The moving average method involves using the average of the most recent data values to forecast the next period.

The number of data values we use to compile our average can be selected in order to minimize the forecasting error – more of this later on page 149.

Let us take a simple example of the weekly sales of flour from a supermarket. The data might look like this:

Table 11.1
Weekly Flour Sales from a Supermarket

Week	Sales (kgs)	Week	Sales (kgs)
1	30	9	31
2	33	10	28
3	29	11	32
4	32	12	35
5	30	13	32
6	32	14	29
7	34	15	31
8	30	16	28

Let us choose to use four data values, that is, base our forecast on a four-week moving average:

Forecast for week 5 = moving average of weeks 1 to 4

$$= \frac{20 + 33 + 29 + 32}{4}$$

$$= 31$$

Since the actual value for week 5 is 30, the forecast error is said to be $30 - 31$, that is, -1.

We go on to forecast week 6, dropping the first week's results and including the result for the fifth week as follows:

Forecast for week 6 = moving average of weeks 2 to 5

$$= \frac{33 + 29 + 32 + 30}{4}$$

$$= 31$$

The forecast error is $32 - 31 = +1$.

We go on repeating the calculation and the results are set out

Table 11.2

Weekly Flour Sales – Four-week Moving Average Forecast

Time	Time Series	Moving Average Forecast	Forecast Error	Forecast Error Squared
1	30			
2	33			
3	29			
4	32			
5	30	31.00	−1.00	1.00
6	32	31.00	+1.00	1.00
7	34	30.75	+3.25	10.56
8	30	32.00	−2.00	4.00
9	31	31.50	−0.50	0.25
10	28	31.75	−3.75	14.06
11	32	30.75	+1.25	1.56
12	35	30.25	+4.75	22.56
13	32	31.50	+0.50	0.25
14	29	31.75	−2.75	7.56
15	31	32.00	−1.00	1.00
16	28	31.75	−3.75	14.06
		Totals	−4.00	77.86

in Table 11.2. The forecast error has been squared to get rid of the minus signs.

The results, shown graphically in Figure 11.3, demonstrate how the moving average smooths out the fluctuations in the original series.

We mentioned forecasting error on page 148 and it would seem that the simple way to work out the overall forecasting error for a series of data would be to take the average of the individual forecasting errors. However, you will see that as some of them are positive and some are negative they tend to cancel each other out. So, instead, we use the average of the squared errors, sometimes referred to as the MEAN SQUARED ERROR. The mean squared error in our example is:

$$\frac{77.86}{12} = 6.49$$

Now, you will remember that we mentioned that we could choose the number of data points to use in our moving average in order

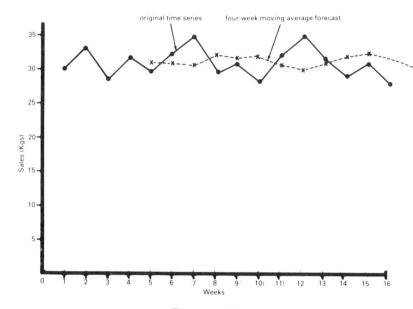

Figure 11.3
*Flour Sales Time Series and Four-week Moving Average
Forecast*

to minimize our forecasting error. So, what we could do is to
repeat the previous calculations for perhaps a three-week or a
five-week moving average and see which gives the smallest forecast
error. We won't do that here!

Trend Projections

In this section we will look at how we forecast from a time series
that shows a long-term linear trend. In fact we use a technique
you are already familiar with – linear regression. Let us consider
some historical data for the production of toasters set out in Table
11.3 and shown graphically in Figure 11.4.

You will recall from page 130 that our linear regression equation
linking a dependent variable y and an independent variable x was:

$$y = a_o + b_o x$$

Table 11.3
Toaster Production

Year	Units (000s)	Year	Units (000s)
1	50	6	54
2	52	7	57
3	56	8	60
4	51	9	62
5	48	10	58

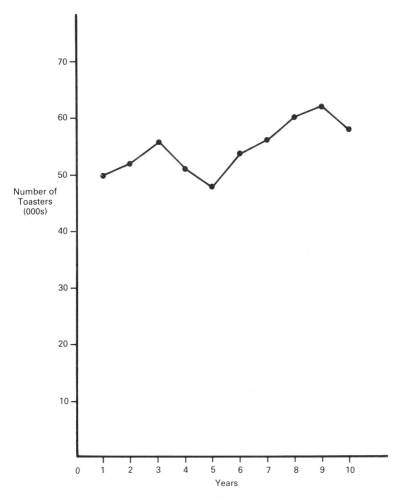

Figure 11.4
Time Series of the Production of Toasters

In order to emphasize that the independent variable is 'time', we will express the equation as follows:

$$y_t = a_o + b_o t$$

where y_t = forecast value of time series in time t
$\quad a_o$ = intercept of the trend line
$\quad b_o$ = slope of the trend line
$\quad t$ = time point.

We can calculate a_o and b_o by the following formulae:

$$b_o = \frac{\Sigma t y_t - (\Sigma t \, \Sigma y_t)/n}{\Sigma t^2 - [(\Sigma t)^2]/n}$$

$$a_o = (\Sigma y_t)/n - b_o(\Sigma t)/n$$

where n = number of data points.

You will remember from page 131 where we introduced linear regression, that it is useful to prepare our data in the following tabular form:

Table 11.4
Toaster Production – Useful Tabulations

t	y_t	$t y_t$	t^2
1	50	50	1
2	52	104	4
3	56	168	9
4	51	204	16
5	48	240	25
6	54	324	36
7	57	399	49
8	60	480	64
9	62	558	81
10	58	580	100
55	548	3107	385

Substituting in the formulae, we have:

$$b_o = \frac{3{,}107 - (55 \times 548)/10}{385 - (55 \times 55)/10}$$

$$= \frac{3{,}107 - 3{,}014}{385 - 302.5}$$

$$= \frac{93}{82.5}$$

$$= 1.13$$

$$a_o = \frac{548}{10} - 1.13 \times \frac{55}{10}$$

$$= 54.8 - 6.22$$

$$= 48.58$$

The equation can be written as:

$$y_t = 48.58 + 1.13t$$

The slope indicates that over the past ten years there has been an increase in production of about 1,130 toasters each year. Figure 11.5 shows the trend line.

If we wanted to forecast production in years 11 and 12 we would calculate it as follows:

$$y_{11} = 48.58 + 1.13 \times 11$$
$$= 48.58 + 12.43$$
$$= 61.01 \text{ (or 61,010 toasters).}$$

and
$$y_{12} = 48.58 + 1.13 \times 12$$
$$= 48.58 + 13.56$$
$$= 62.14 \text{ (or 62,140 toasters)}$$

and so we could go on.

Remember, this method assumes that we have a linear, or straight line, trend and that the future will be like the past. As you will remember from our introduction to trends, there are several different types of trend but it is not the intention in this book to explain how to cope with non-linear trends.

Forecasting with Seasonal Elements

So far we have covered how to forecast from a time series where there are no significant trends, cyclical or seasonal elements, using the *moving averages* smoothing method. Then, we looked at how we forecast from a time series which displayed a long term linear trend, using linear regression techniques. Now we are going to

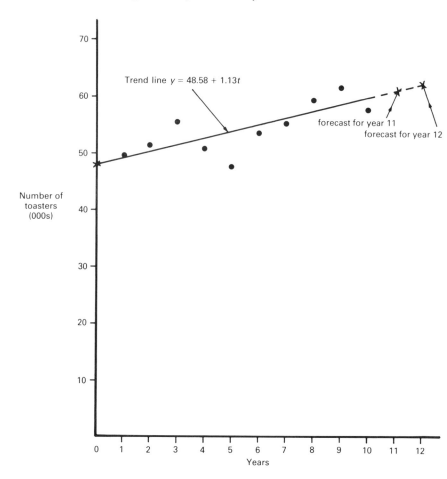

Figure 11.5
*Trend Line of the Production of Toasters – Giving Forecasts
for Years 11 and 12*

explain a little about how to tackle a time series which has both a trend and a seasonal element.

We are going to use what is known as the multiplicative model which assumes that a time series value (Y) can be formed by multiplying the trend element (T), the seasonal element (S) and the irregular element (I) as follows:

$$Y = T \times S \times I$$

T is expressed in units of the item being forecast. However, *S* and *I* are measured in relative terms, with values above 1 showing a seasonal or irregular effect *above* the trend, and values below 1 showing a seasonal or irregular effect *below* the trend. For example, assume that we have a trend forecast of 100 units for a particular time period and values of *S* and *I* equal to 1.10 and 0.97 respectively. Then, for that period, the value of the time series is:

$$Y = 100 \times 1.10 \times 0.97$$
$$= 106.7$$

The first stage in our forecasting procedure is to calculate the seasonal factors. This is a quite straightforward if somewhat lengthy process. It involves smoothing out our time series using the method discussed earlier in this chapter, but with one variation. We work out what are known as *centred moving averages*, which are simply averages of the moving averages. Dividing our original observations by the equivalent centred moving averages gives us a seasonal factor for each observation. Then we take the seasonal factors for a quarter, for example the 1st quarter, and average them to remove the irregular elements. Hence we arrive at seasonal factors for each of the four quarters.

Let us look at a specific example in an area of interest to many managers, that of the energy consumption of a company, often measured in gigajoules (a term which allows all energy requirements to be expressed by a common unit regardless of whether they are provided by electricity, coal, gas, etc.). The data is given in Table 11.5.

The time series graph of our original observations together with the centred moving averages is shown in Figure 11.6.

Using the process described above we obtain the following seasonal factors:

1st quarter	1.145
2nd quarter	0.983
3rd quarter	0.845
4th quarter	1.027

This shows us that the highest consumption is in the first quarter and is about 14% above the average quarterly value. The lowest level of consumption is in the third quarter and is nearly 16%

Table 11.5
Energy Consumption of a Company

Year	Quarter	Energy Consumption (000s gigajoules)	Year	Quarter	Energy Consumption (000s gigajoules)
1	1	100	4	1	120
	2	80		2	111
	3	70		3	100
	4	90		4	115
2	1	110	5	1	130
	2	93		2	120
	3	98		3	108
	4	100		4	122
3	1	115			
	2	100			
	3	90			
	4	110			

below the quarterly average. The second and fourth quarters show consumption very close (within 3%) to the quarterly average.

We are now ready to go on to the next stage. Let us go back to our model:

$$Y = T \times S \times I$$

Re-write it as:

$$T \times I = \frac{Y}{S}$$

The trend/irregular element $(T \times I)$ can be calculated by dividing each observation by the appropriate seasonal factor. This process is called DE-SEASONALIZING the time series.

We can now plot the de-seasonalized trend line, using the de-seasonalized figures rather than the original observations. Note the difference in Figure 11.7.

Now, although the graph has some fluctuations there is a discernible trend which we can go on to calculate as we did previously (pages 128–34), using linear regression. This time, however, we are using the de-seasonalized results rather than the original observations. The trend equation can be solved to give

$$T = 80.4 + 2.2t \text{ (see Figure 11.8).}$$

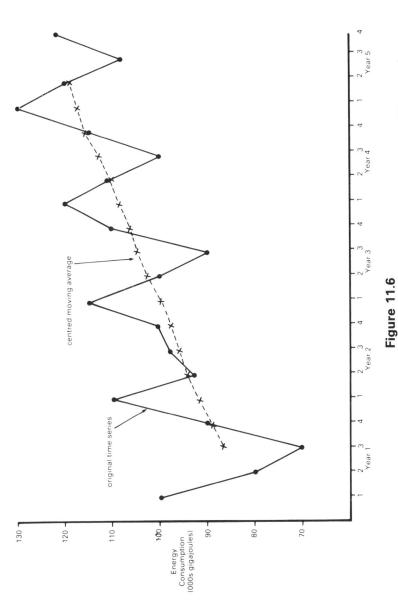

Figure 11.6

Time Series of a Company's Energy Consumption and Four-quarterly Centred Moving Average

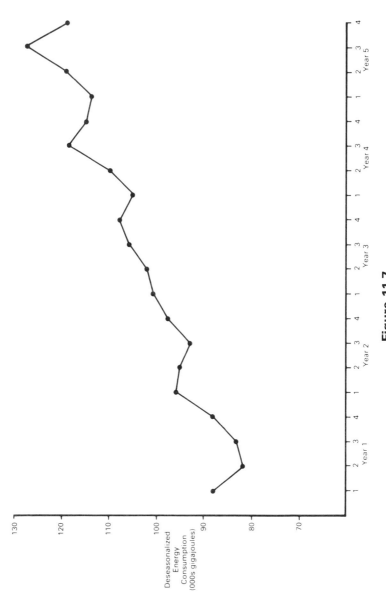

Figure 11.7
Deseasonalized Energy Consumption

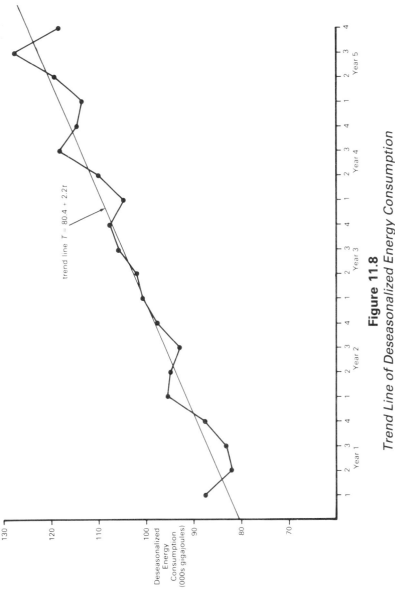

Figure 11.8

Trend Line of Deseasonalized Energy Consumption

The slope of 2.2 indicates that over the past five years or twenty quarters, the company has experienced an average de-seasonalized increase in energy consumption of 2.2 thousand gigajoules per quarter.

So, if we want to forecast the trend element for the first quarter of year 6, that is the 21st quarter, we use our trend equation:

$$T = 80.4 + 2.2 \times 21$$
$$= 126.6$$

We then apply the seasonal factor for the first quarter to get our forecast:

$$T = 126.6 \times 1.145$$
$$= 145.0$$

In the same way, we can go on to forecast future quarters. This must have seemed a rather complex set of calculations. However, it is quite simple really – we just need to follow each step. First we smoothed the data to identify the seasonal elements for each quarter. We then went on to identify the trend by working out the linear regression equation for the de-seasonalized results. We use this trend equation to forecast our trend element and then apply the appropriate quarterly seasonal factor to arrive at our final forecast.

So far we have discussed quarterly data; however, we might often have data for a different time interval, perhaps monthly. The approach is identical except that a 12-month moving average replaces the quarterly moving average and we go on to identify twelve seasonal factors.

Conclusion

So, there you have it – time series analysis and forecasting – all quite simple, as we promised. However, all the quantitative methods are critically dependent on the belief that the future will be an extension of the past. Unfortunately for statisticians, this is not always the case and we must constantly bear that in mind. The further ahead we try and forecast, the less relevant can be the past trends. As ever, in pursuing the statistical technique we must never suspend our professional judgement about the meaningfulness of the results of our calculations and therefore, in the ultimate, the use to which these results can be put.

12

Index Numbers, Published Indices and Sources of Data

Introduction

INDEX NUMBERS are used to measure changes over time. Rather than simply presenting the data as a series of observations measured over time it is often clearer and more useful to present them in index number form. This means presenting the data as a proportion or percentage of some base value. For example, suppose we have two factories producing radios and their performance, as measured by the number of radios manufactured, is as follows:

	1986	*1987*	*1988*	*1989*
Factory A	1,500	1,600	1,800	2,200
Factory B	4,000	4,500	4,600	5,000

It is very difficult to see which factory has improved its performance most. So, we will express these results as index numbers, using 1986 as the base year. To do this we divide each result by the result for 1986 as shown below. (Alternatively, the index numbers can be presented in percentage form, by multiplying by 100.)

	1986	*1987*	*1988*	*1989*
Factory A	$\dfrac{1,500}{1,500}$	$\dfrac{1,600}{1,500}$	$\dfrac{1,800}{1,500}$	$\dfrac{2,200}{1,500}$
	$= 1.00$	$= 1.067$	$= 1.200$	$= 1.467$
Factory B	$\dfrac{4,000}{4,000}$	$\dfrac{4,500}{4,000}$	$\dfrac{4,600}{4,000}$	$\dfrac{5,000}{4,000}$
	$= 1.00$	$= 1.125$	$= 1.150$	$= 1.250$

Although Factory B is making 1,000 more radios in 1989 than in 1986, whereas Factory A is making only 700 more, it is clear from using index numbers that Factory A's increase in performance, at 46.7%, is superior to that of Factory B where performance has increased by only 25%.

The usefulness of index numbers become even more marked when we are trying to compare unlike items. For example, suppose Factory A makes bottles and Factory B makes cars:

	1986	1987	1988	1989
Factory A (Bottles)	10,000	12,000	13,000	16,000
Factory B (Cars)	500	650	800	900

It is meaningless to try and compare the actual increase in bottles with the actual increase in cars – how do you judge an increase of 6,000 bottles against an increase of 400 cars?

Well, what about turning them into common units, for example the money value of production? This could help, but this approach could cause as many problems as it solves! We will look at this suggestion shortly, but first let us look at the increases in terms of an index of units based on 1986. The results are:

	1986	1987	1988	1989
Factory A (Bottles)	1.0	1.2	1.3	1.6
Factory B (Cars)	1.0	1.3	1.6	1.8

Clearly Factory B is increasing production at a faster rate than Factory A.

Let us now look at the example, as suggested earlier, in terms of the value of production. Suppose that the value of a bottle is 25p and the value of a car is £10,000 *and* these values remain constant over time. The results are:

Value of Production (£)

	1986	1987	1988	1989
Factory A (Bottles)	2,500	3,000	3,250	4,000
Factory B (Cars)	5,000,000	6,500,000	8,000,000	9,000,000

We can express the increase in value of production as an index based on 1986. The results are as follows:

	1986	1987	1988	1989
Factory A (Bottles)	1.0	1.2	1.3	1.6
Factory B (Cars)	1.0	1.3	1.6	1.8

Yes, the index numbers are the same as we obtained above.

However, let us suppose the unit value of the bottle has increased as follows:

1986	1987	1988	1989
25p	30p	40p	50p

and the unit value of the car has increased as follows:

1986	1987	1988	1989
10,000	11,000	12,000	13,000

Now the value of production (£) is:

	1986	1987	1988	1989
Factory A (Bottles)	2,500	3,600	5,200	8,000
Factory B (Cars)	5,000,000	7,150,000	9,600,000	11,700,000

It can also be expressed as index numbers with 1986 as the base year:

	1986	1987	1988	1989
Factory A (Bottles)	1.00	1.44	2.08	3.20
Factory B (Cars)	1.00	1.43	1.92	2.34

The picture has changed: Factory A appears to be performing better, but is it? No, the answer has been clouded by the price increase. Factory A has not increased its productivity more than Factory B, it has merely benefited from a steeper price increase. So we must be very careful when we make such comparisons, that we understand *what* we are comparing and *what* conclusions can be drawn. In the next section we consider this business of the changing value of money as we look at one of the most well known and useful indices, the Retail Prices Index (RPI).

Retail Prices Index (RPI)

The Retail Prices Index is probably the most important and useful published index. It is certainly the one most often quoted in the media. After the period of very high price inflation in the 1970s it is now seen as an important indicator of how well the economy is doing. It is probably the only economic indicator that is readily understood and appreciated by the non-economist as people can see the direct impact on their financial well-being.

What does the RPI do? It purports to measure the change in prices over a period of time (and is presented in the percentage form of an index). The base year is revised at regular intervals to maintain it as a readily understood set of indices. It was revised in January 1974 and again in January 1987. These months became the base points for subsequent years. The RPI is designed to try and measure changes in prices in an average or representative *basket* of goods and services. There are eleven main categories in the basket:

Food
Alcoholic drink
Tobacco
Housing
Fuel and lighting
Durable household goods
Clothing and footwear
Transport and vehicles
Miscellaneous food
Services
Meals bought and consumed outside the home.

Within each category there is a vast range of individual items. Something of the order of 350 items are selected each month for price investigation. Basically a sample of prices is taken from different areas and different types of stores. From these it is possible to estimate individual indices. How then do we arrive at one figure – one index number? A simple way would be to take a straight average, that is, take all the different index numbers based on the same year, add them together and divide by the number of categories.

So let's take a simplified example. Suppose we have three items

(*A*, *B* and *C*) with indices for January 1988 based on January 1985:

$$I_A = 110$$
$$I_B = 130$$
$$I_C = 140$$

$$\text{Simple average} = \frac{110 + 130 + 140}{3}$$
$$= \frac{380}{3}$$
$$= 126.7$$

This would only be appropriate if each of the separate indices was equally important. However, it is quite obvious that changes in housing prices will have a much greater impact on the population at large than changes in tobacco or alcoholic drinks because people spend very much more on housing than on tobacco or alcoholic drinks. Therefore, in order to arrive at a true average, it is necessary to weight the different components. Going back to our simple example, let us suppose that the average family spends 50% of its income on item *A*, 30% on item *B* and 20% on item *C*.

$$\text{Weighted average} = 110 \times \frac{50}{100} + 130 \times \frac{30}{100} + 140 \times \frac{20}{100}$$
$$= 110 \times 0.5 + 130 \times 0.3 + 140 \times 0.2$$
$$= 55 + 39 + 28$$
$$= 122$$

The weighted average is less than the simple average, reflecting that the price increase in the most important item, Item *A*, is rather less than the other two items. The Government Statisticians use the results of another survey, the Family Expenditure Survey, to arrive at the different weighting factors to apply. This survey examines expenditure patterns of a sample of households.

Set out in Table 12.1 is the Retail Prices Index from 1974 to the end of 1988. It can be seen that it provides monthly indices and average annual indices between 1974 and 1988, and that it has been re-based in 1987. So, how do we work out a particular increase in prices? Let's look at some examples:

Table 12.1
Retail Prices Index, 1974–1988

GENERAL INDEX OF RETAIL PRICES (Prices at January 1974=100)

Year	Jan	Feb	Mar	Apr	May	June	July	Aug	Sept	Oct	Nov	Dec	Annual Average
1974	100.0	101.7	102.6	106.1	107.6	108.7	109.7	109.8	111.0	113.2	115.2	116.9	108.5
1975	119.9	121.9	124.3	129.1	134.5	137.1	138.5	139.3	140.5	142.5	144.2	146.0	134.8
1976	147.9	149.8	150.6	153.5	155.2	156.0	156.3	158.5	160.6	163.5	165.8	168.0	157.1
1977	172.4	174.1	175.8	180.3	181.7	183.6	183.8	184.7	185.7	186.5	187.4	188.4	182.0
1978	189.5	190.6	191.8	194.6	195.7	197.2	198.1	199.4	200.2	201.1	202.5	204.2	197.1
1979	207.2	208.9	210.6	214.2	215.9	219.6	229.1	230.9	233.2	235.6	237.7	239.4	223.5
1980	245.3	248.8	252.2	260.8	263.2	265.7	267.9	268.5	270.2	271.9	274.1	275.6	263.7
1981	277.3	279.8	284.0	292.2	294.1	295.8	297.1	299.3	301.0	303.7	306.9	308.8	295.0
1982	310.6	310.7	313.4	319.7	322.0	322.9	323.0	323.1	322.9	324.5	326.1	325.5	320.4
1983	325.9	327.3	327.9	332.5	333.9	334.7	336.5	338.0	339.5	340.7	341.9	342.8	335.1
1984	342.6	344.0	345.1	349.7	351.0	351.9	351.5	354.8	355.5	357.7	358.8	358.5	351.8
1985	359.8	362.7	366.1	373.9	375.6	376.4	375.7	376.7	376.5	377.1	378.4	378.9	373.2
1986	379.7	381.1	381.6	385.3	386.0	385.8	384.7	385.9	387.8	388.4	391.7	393.0	385.9
1987	394.5	396.1	396.9	401.6	402.0	402.0	401.6	402.8	404.0	405.9	407.9	407.5	402.0

GENERAL INDEX OF RETAIL PRICES (Prices at January 1987=100)

Year	Jan	Feb	Mar	Apr	May	June	July	Aug	Sept	Oct	Nov	Dec	Annual Average
1987	100.0	100.4	100.6	101.8	101.9	101.9	101.8	102.1	102.4	102.9	103.4	103.3	101.9
1988	103.3	103.7	104.1	105.8	106.2	106.6	106.7	107.9	108.4	109.5	110.0	110.3	106.9

The figures in the lower table may be linked to the one above by multiplying the figures in the lower table by 3.945.

a   What is the price increase between January 1975 and June 1979?

> Index for January 1975   = 119.9
> Index for June 1979   = 219.6

We want the June 1979 index based on January 1975, that is, the index when January 1975 = 100, so we divide each index by 1.199:

> Index for January 1975
> (Based on Jan $= \dfrac{119.9}{1.199} = 100.0$
> 1975 = 100)
>
> Index for June 1979
> (Based on Jan $= \dfrac{219.6}{1.199} = 183.2$
> 1975 = 100)

Therefore prices have increased by 83.2% over the period January 1975 to June 1979.

b   What is the price increase between May 1976 and February 1984?

> Index for May 1976   = 155.2
> Index for February 1984 = 344.0

Again, we want the February 1984 index based on May 1976, that is the index when May 1976 = 100, so we divide each index by 1.552:

> Index for May 1976
> (Based on May 1976 $= \dfrac{155.2}{1.552} = 100.0$
>   = 100)
>
> Index for February 1984 $= \dfrac{344.0}{1.552} = 221.7$
> (Based on May 1976 = 100)

Therefore prices have increased by 121.7% over the period May 1976 to February 1984.

c   What is the price increase between March 1985 and December 1988?

This is a little trickier as the index was re-based in 1987. The index number for January 1987, with January 1974 as the base year, is 394.5. To get index numbers based on January 1987 as 100 we therefore divide by 3.945. To go the other way, that is, from an index based on January 1987 = 100 to January 1974 = 100, we multiply the index number by 3.945 as follows:

$$\frac{\text{Index for December 1988}}{\text{(Based on Jan 1987 = 100)}} = 110.3$$

$$\frac{\text{Index for December 1988}}{\text{(Based on Jan 1974 = 100)}} = 110.3 \times 3.945$$

$$= 435.1$$

$$\frac{\text{Index for March 1985}}{\text{(Based on Jan 1974 = 100)}} = 366.1$$

Next we calculate March 1985 as our new base point, converting it to 100 by dividing by 3.661:

$$\frac{\text{Index for March 1985}}{\text{(Based on Mar 1985 = 100)}} = \frac{366.1}{3.661} = 100.0$$

$$\frac{\text{Index for December 1988}}{\text{(Based on Mar 1985 = 100)}} = \frac{435.1}{3.661} = 118.8$$

Therefore prices have increased by 18.8% over the period March 1985 to December 1988.

d   What is the price increase between 1980 and 1985? Here we use the annual average and in fact these are probably most frequently used and quoted. The calculations are just the same as before:

Average index for 1980   = 263.7
Average index for 1985   = 373.2

As we want the 1985 index to be based on 1980, we divide each index by 2.637:

$$\frac{\text{Index for 1980}}{\text{(Based on 1980 = 100)}} = \frac{263.7}{2.637} = 100.0$$

$$\frac{\text{Index for 1985}}{\text{(Based on 1980 = 100)}} = \frac{373.2}{2.637} = 141.5$$

Therefore prices have increased by 41.5% between 1980 and 1985.

So, as we have seen, it is quite simple to manipulate the indices to get the information we want, but how might we use this information?

Use of the Retail Prices Index

The Retail Prices Index is a vital tool when we want to look at the trend in data over time which is affected by price increases. An obvious example is earnings – suppose we want to look at how the earnings of our workforce have increased after allowing for inflation, or increased *in real terms*, which is the phrase commonly used. Suppose average earnings had moved in actual terms and expressed as an index based on 1980 = 100, as follows:

Table 12.2
Average Earnings Index

Year	Earnings (£,000)	Index
1980	3,000	100
1981	3,300	110
1982	4,000	133
1983	4,700	157
1984	5,500	183
1985	6,000	200
1986	6,300	210
1987	6,700	223
1988	7,200	240

Over the whole period, earnings have apparently increased in money terms (that is, not adjusted for price inflation) by 140%.

Now let us adjust for price inflation using the RPI. There are two ways of doing this, both basically the same – either express all the earnings at 1980 prices or at 1988 prices. In fact we could express them in any price year, as long as we are consistent. Let's do it in terms of 1980 prices, and choose January 1980 as the base period. We multiply each year's earnings by:

$$\frac{\text{the RPI in January 1980}}{\text{the RPI in January of that year}}$$

The results are shown in Table 12.3.

By using the RPI we get quite a different picture. Overall real earnings have increased by only 44% in the eight years. In the first year, in real terms, they actually declined. This was because although the employees' earnings rose by 10%, inflation rose by 13% (277.3 ÷ 245.3). Then, between 1985 and 1987, in real terms, earnings were virtually static. As you will appreciate, the trade

Table 12.3
Earnings Adjusted for Price Inflation

Year	Actual Earnings	RPI (Jan)	Earnings at 1980 Prices	Index Numbers
1980	3,000	245.3	$3,000 \times 245.3 \div 245.3 = 3,000$	100
1981	3,300	277.3	$3,300 \times 245.3 \div 277.3 = 2,919$	97
1982	4,000	310.6	$4,000 \times 245.3 \div 310.6 = 3,159$	105
1983	4,700	325.9	$4,700 \times 245.3 \div 325.9 = 3,538$	118
1984	5,500	342.6	$5,500 \times 245.3 \div 342.6 = 3,938$	131
1985	6,000	359.8	$6,000 \times 245.3 \div 359.8 = 4,091$	136
1986	6,300	379.7	$6,300 \times 245.3 \div 379.7 = 4,070$	136
1987	6,700	394.5	$6,700 \times 245.3 \div 394.5 = 4,166$	139
1988	7,200	407.5	$7,200 \times 245.3 \div 407.5 = 4,334$	144

unions are far keener to talk about real earnings than actual earnings!

Let's take another example. Suppose you are the manager of a department store and you measure your performance by sales. However, you are really interested to know how your sales have increased in real terms, or what the *volume* sales increase is (as opposed to the sales value increase in actual money terms). This time we will express our sales in terms of the latest year, 1988, and use the average annual indices. So we multiply the sales figures by:

$$\frac{\text{the RPI in 1988}}{\text{the RPI in that year}}$$

Table 12.4
Sales Volumes

Year	Actual Sales (£m)	RPI (annual average)	Sales at 1988 Prices (£m)	Index Numbers
1984	20	351.8	$20 \times 421.8 \div 351.8 = 24.0$	100
1985	25	373.2	$25 \times 421.8 \div 373.2 = 28.3$	118
1986	27	385.9	$27 \times 421.8 \div 385.9 = 29.5$	123
1987	30	402.0	$30 \times 421.8 \div 402.0 = 31.5$	131
1988	36	421.8	$36 \times 421.8 \div 421.8 = 36.0$	150

Therefore, over the period 1984 to 1988, sales have increased in volume by some 50%.

We hope you have begun to see just how useful the RPI is. The main source is the Department of Employment Gazette, which is published monthly. There are other price indices available, geared towards particular sectors. Two of the most commonly referred to are:

a   The Wholesale Prices Index which measures the prices that producers have to pay for inputs such as raw materials and fuel. It is a producers' price index rather than a consumers' price index like the RPI. As the price of inputs eventually feed through to the finished product and consumer prices, the Wholesale Prices Index is often seen as an early warning of changes in inflation levels.

b   The Construction Prices Indices which measure the changes of prices in construction work. There are a number of different indices which are used to adjust the prices of contracts for inflation.

Stock Market Indices

Another set of well known and regularly quoted indices are those applying to the stock market. Stock market indices tell us the movement over time in aggregate share prices, or the prices of other securities. In Great Britain the most widely used and best known are those published by the Financial Times (FT). They are of three types – the FT-Ordinary (or 30 Share) Index, the FT-Actuaries Indices and the FT-Stock Exchange 100 Index. Their method of calculation and uses are quite different.

The FT-Ordinary Index was started in 1935 and is the one which gets the most publicity. It is a price index of the shares of thirty premier industrial, financial and commercial companies in the UK. The companies are leaders in their fields and are selected to give a wide coverage of industries together representing a relatively large part of the stock market as a whole. The index of 100 represents this average at the base date of 1 July 1935. The Index is calculated every hour, on the hour, between 10.00am and 4.00pm, and at the close around 5.00pm.

The FT-Actuaries Share Indices are designed to measure particular portfolio performance. There are over thirty groups or subsections and they are compiled jointly by the Financial Times, the Institute of Actuaries and the Faculty of Actuaries. The Indices' main function is to serve as a reliable measure of portfolio performance. The FT-Actuaries All Share Index represents over three quarters of the total market value of shares on the Stock Exchange.

The FT-SE 100 Index was designed to meet the need for an index which would cover options and futures contracts based on the UK market. The basis of calculation of the FT-SE 100 Index is very similar to that of the All Share Index, but based, as the name suggests, on only 100 companies. The Index is re-calculated almost continuously throughout the day from 9.30am to well after the official close. The base level was set at 1,000 at the end of business on 30 December 1983.

There are other Indices published by the Financial Times for specific purposes, and by overseas organizations. These latter ones should be used with caution because they are not all calculated in the same way. One of the best known of the foreign indices is the Dow Jones Industrial Average. This is an un-weighted arithmetic average of thirty leading shares on the New York Stock Exchange.

Sources of Data

There are three main sources of data and one could write a textbook on each of them. However, we will restrict ourselves to a brief outline of what we believe are some of the most useful sources from:

a   Government statistical publications;
b   private market research surveys;
c   information from within and about individual organizations.

Government Statistical Publications

General Information. General information is set out in the following publications:

a   *Monthly Digest of Statistics* – a collection of the main sources of statistics from all Government departments.

b   *Annual Abstract of Statistics* – contains more series of data than the *Monthly Digest* and a greater run of years.
c   *Social Trends* – includes key social and demographic series (annual).

Population and Households. Population and household information is available from:

a   *Census* – a full census is carried out at regular intervals; the last one was in 1981, giving information across a whole range of subjects, for example, household composition, income, transport to work, etc.
b   *Family Expenditure Survey* – sets out the income and expenditure in a detailed form by type of household (annual).
c   *General Household Survey* – a continuous sample survey of households covering a wide range of social and economic policy areas.

Manpower/Earnings/Retail Prices. Details on manpower, earnings and retail prices are set out in:

a   *Department of Employment Gazette* – includes information on employment/unemployment, hours worked, earnings, labour costs and retail prices, etc. (monthly).
b   *New Earnings Survey* – relates to earnings from employment by industry category, at April each year.

General Economy. General economic statistics are set out in:

a   *Economic Trends* – a useful selection of tables and charts on the United Kingdom economy (monthly).
b   *UK National Accounts* (*Blue Book*) – give detailed estimates (annual). It is a bit heavy going for most people but is beloved by economists.

Industrial Production and Sales. Details on industrial production and sales are reported in the Census of Production (annual) – available by industry and in summary form. Data is included on total purchases, sales, stocks, work in progress, capital expenditure, employment, etc.

Private Market Research

There are numerous surveys carried out regularly by private agencies. Some of the ones with which we are most familiar are:

a income and earnings surveys;
b public opinion surveys on such topics as the state of the UK political parties, our views on the environment, etc.;
c surveys aimed at particular industries or products, for example, the *Which?* consumer surveys on cars.

Organization Information

There are three excellent sources of information on individual organizations:

a The Annual Report and Accounts published by all large companies. Often these are glossy brochures and, apart from giving financial information on the company, will also provide background information on the company's products, work-force, markets, expansion plans, etc.
b Stock broker bulletins – the City brokers regularly produce bulletins on companies for their investors. Again, although biased towards the investor, they usually provide a very useful appraisal of that company.
c Newspaper articles – particularly from *The Financial Times* and other quality newspapers – usually provide an easy-to-read, potted summary of the company. They are usually produced around the time of the company's results being announced or when there is some particular interest in the company – perhaps there is a takeover bid or the company has diversified in some way. Some large libraries, for example, the City Business Library, carry a very useful reference set of such articles – called McCarthy Cards – indexed by company name.

Conclusion

We hope that our brief discussion of index numbers has given you a feel for this very useful topic. Together with the rich and varied sources of information detailed above, it should help you to get to grips with analysing and understanding organizations and their happenings. If in doubt about sources of information, a good place to start is the research library of your own organization, where such a facility exists. Otherwise your local college/polytechnic/university library, or the local public library, will contain a surprising amount of information and have very helpful staff who know where to find it for you.

13

Decision Theory

Introduction

DECISION THEORY is a rather good name for what is quite a simple and straightforward approach to decision making. Decision theory or, as it is sometimes called, decision analysis is used to arrive at an optimal (best) strategy when faced with a number of alternative strategies or decisions and an uncertain future. Take a very simple example, suppose we are buyers for a clothes shop and we need to decide in the Autumn how much rainwear to buy for the Spring. Clearly if it is wet, Spring and Summer demand will be great, but if the sun shines a lot, the demand will be limited. On the one hand we want to buy enough to meet demand and gain maximum profits. On the other hand, we do not want to buy too much, as this could lead to us having stock on our hands at the end of the season which we have to reduce in price to sell. How do we decide what to buy so far in advance? We cannot know for certain what the weather is going to be like so far ahead. We will look at a simple way of structuring the decisions using the technique of a payoff table.

Payoff Tables

The best way to explain decision theory is to take an example. Suppose we are furniture manufacturers and we want to build a new factory. We have the choice of building a small, a medium or a large factory. We, therefore, have three decision choices which we will label d_1, d_2 and d_3:

$$d_1 = \text{build a small factory}$$
$$d_2 = \text{build a medium factory}$$
$$d_3 = \text{build a large factory}$$

Our decision will be based on how we see the future market for our product. In this simple example suppose there are two possible outcomes – a high demand or a low demand for our furniture. If we build our factory too small and demand is high we will lose sales and profit. However, if we build our factory too large and demand is low, then we will have expensive spare capacity on our hands and potential losses. So, let us label our two outcomes o_1 and o_2:

$$o_1 = \text{low demand}$$
$$o_2 = \text{high demand}$$

The next step is to estimate the payoffs for each combination of decision and outcome. In this case payoff would be measured in terms of profit and we can construct a PAYOFF TABLE for this decision making problem as follows:

Decision Choices	*Outcomes*	
	Low Demand	*High Demand*
	o_1	o_2
Build a small factory d_1	£20,000	£50,000
Build a medium factory d_2	£10,000	£80,000
Build a large factory d_3	−£10,000	£100,000

The figures in the above payoff table are our best estimates of what the profit might be under the different circumstances. In a commercial situation it is possible that we would have some idea of what the demand might be – in other words, we would have a good idea as to how probable it is that there would be a high demand or a low demand. However, let us assume that we have no confidence in our view of the future, so we will need some criteria against which to make our decision. Let us look at two of these – the MAXIMIN/MINIMAX criterion and the MAXIMAX/MINIMIN criterion.

Maximin/Minimax

The maximin decision criterion is the pessimistic, or conservative, approach to arriving at a decision. As the name suggests, we maximize the minimum possible payoffs or, in our case, profits.

Take the figures from the table above and list the minimum payoff for each decision:

Decision Choices	Minimum Payoff
Build a small factory d_1	£20,000
Build a medium factory d_2	£10,000
Build a large factory d_3	−£10,000

We then choose the decision which gives us the maximum of the minimum payoffs. In this example we would choose d_1 – to build a small factory.

If our payoff table was constructed on the basis of costs rather than profit, we would reverse the criterion to minimax, that is, we would choose the minimum from the list of maximum costs related to each decision.

Maximax/Minimin

While maximin and minimax offer pessimistic decision criteria, maximax does quite the opposite – it provides an optimistic criterion. Let us take our example again from the above table but this time list the maximum payoffs for each decision:

Decision Choices	Maximum Payoff
Build a small factory d_1	£50,000
Build a medium factory d_2	£80,000
Build a large factory d_3	£100,000

We select the decision which gives the maximum payoff – in this case we would decide to build a large factory. Again, if we are dealing with a payoff table of costs, we would reverse the criterion and use a minimin criterion.

Expected Monetary Value

We will now look at the slightly more complex but very useful technique for making decisions where you have some expectation, or can apply some probability to the outcomes:

Suppose we have a number n of decision alternatives:

$$d_1, d_2, \ldots, d_n$$

and a number N of outcomes

$$o_1, o_2, \ldots, o_N$$

Suppose also:

p_1 = probability of outcome o_1 occurring
p_2 = probability of outcome o_2 occurring
.
.
.
p_N = probability of outcome o_N occurring

You will recall from page 83 in the chapter on probability that:

$$p_i \geqslant 0 \text{ for all outcomes, and}$$
$$p_1 + p_2 + \ldots + p_N = 1$$

The EXPECTED MONETARY VALUE of a decision is the sum of the weighted payoffs for each outcome, with the weights being the probability of that payoff or outcome occurring.

Therefore, the expected monetary value (EMV) of decision d_i

$= p_1 \times$ payoff for decision i and outcome 1
$+ p_2 \times$ payoff for decision i and outcome 2
.
.
.
$+ p_N \times$ payoff for decision i and outcome N

Using this formula and our factory example, let us assume that there is a probability of 0.4 that low demand will be the outcome, and a probability of 0.6 that high demand will be the outcome, then:

EMV of decision d_1 = 0.4 × 20,000 + 0.6 × 50,000 = £38,000
EMV of decision d_2 = 0.4 × 10,000 + 0.6 × 80,000 = £52,000
EMV of decision d_3 = 0.4 × (−10,000) + 0.6 × 100,000
$$= £56,000$$

The criterion for selection is the decision with the highest expected monetary value – in our case, d_3.

If the probabilities are reversed, that is, the probability for low demand is 0.6 and for high demand is 0.4, then the calculation produces the following EMVs:

EMV of decision $d_1 = 0.6 \times 20{,}000 + 0.4 \times 50{,}000 = £32{,}000$
EMV of decision $d_2 = 0.6 \times 10{,}000 + 0.4 \times 80{,}000 = £38{,}000$
EMV of decision $d_3 = 0.6 \times (-10{,}000) + 0.4 \times 100{,}000$
$$= £34{,}000$$

Now the decision to be taken is d_2 – to build a medium factory.

It can be seen that the choice of decision is critically dependent on the probabilities of the different outcomes occurring. More of this later, but let us now take a look at a way of analysing decision making problems graphically using a decision tree.

Decision Trees

You will remember that in Chapter 7 we used a tree diagram to visualize a multi-step experiment of tossing a coin twice. We use a similar diagram here to help in the solution of decision making problems. We can re-express our furniture factory problem, using a DECISION TREE, in the following way:

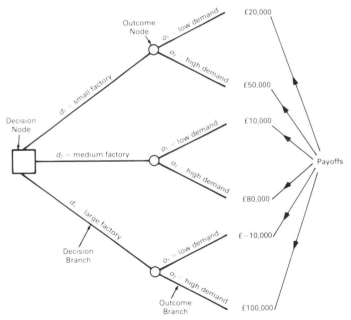

Figure 13.1
Decision Tree of Factory Problem

The tree is made up of nodes:

    – decision nodes;
    – outcome nodes;

and branches:

    – decision branches;
    – outcome branches.

If we now add in the probabilities of the outcomes, being, for example, 0.4 for low demand and 0.6 for high demand, then the tree looks like Figure 13.2:

We work backwards through the tree:

EMV of node 2 = 0.4 × 20,000 + 0.6 × 50,000 = £38,000
(Same as EMV of d_1)
EMV of node 3 = 0.4 × 10,000 + 0.6 × 80,000 = £52,000
(Same as EMV of d_2)
EMV of node 4 = 0.4 × −10,000 + 0.6 × 100,000
(Same as EMV of d_3)   = £56,000

We work backwards again and now have the decision tree which is shown in Figure 13.3.

It can be seen that the best decision is again d_3 – exactly the same as using the expected monetary value criteria and the payoff table – the decision tree is really just a graphical representation of the payoff table.

We have noted the importance of the probabilities of the outcomes. How do we arrive at them? Well, there are several ways, for example, we might look at what has happened in similar circumstances in the past or we might carry out a market research survey. It is even possible to work out how much it is worth paying for information on probabilities.

Risk and Utility

Another area of decision making concerns the decision maker's attitude to risk. Suppose we are faced with the choice of two investments – investment x will provide us with a definite return of £10,000; investment y will provide us with a fifty/fifty chance of £30,000 or nothing:

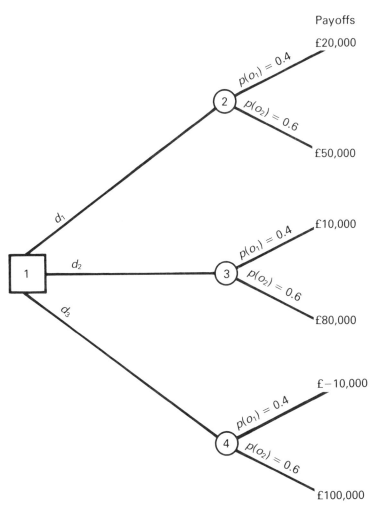

Figure 13.2
Decision Tree of Factory Problem showing Probabilities of the Outcomes

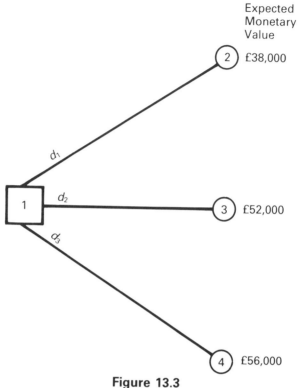

Figure 13.3
*Decision Tree of Factory Problem showing Expected
Monetary Values of the Decisions*

$$\text{EMV }(x) = 10,000$$
$$\text{EMV }(y) = 0.5 \times 30,000 + 0.5 \times 0 = 15,000$$

Based on our earlier criterion we should choose investment y. However, it is quite likely that the investor would choose investment x. We see creeping in here the preference of the decision maker. Investment x is said to have a higher utility – utility being a measure of the decision maker's preference which takes into account not just the expected monetary value but the risks involved.

The concept of utility is particularly useful where there is no strict money value, like profits or costs, associated with an outcome.

There are some interesting examples of this in the field of medicine and to demonstrate the contribution that decision theory can make to dealing with such problems, let's look at the very difficult decision which faces older pregnant women. The risk of Down's Syndrome and other disorders increases with age but can be identified prior to birth by using a test called an amniocentesis test. However, there is a small risk of miscarriage with the test. So here we have a classic decision making situation with known probabilities of the risks. It is impossible to set monetary values on the outcomes – each set of prospective parents will have their own set of utilities, that is, what it would mean to them to have a miscarriage or a handicapped child. A very difficult decision – but one which sometimes can be helped using the decision analysis technique.

Conclusion

So, you have seen that decision theory is quite easy. Although we have tackled it at a simple level, the concepts can be applied widely and to more complex situations. In essence, it is a way of approaching and structuring the decision making process in a logical and systematic way, using some pre-determined criteria. Try using it in some of your everyday situations and see which criterion suits you, what is your attitude to risk and what are your utilities.

Part 3

Computers and Their Applications

'Power to the People'

Having, hopefully, dispelled some of the mystique of statistics and demonstrated how useful these techniques can be, we now introduce you to another world which has tended to be dominated by the experts and their attendant jargon – information technology. Although information technology set off in this way, it is now rapidly becoming an integral part of everyone's working environment.

In Chapter 14 we introduce the computer to those with little knowledge and experience of these machines. We describe what they are and how they work. Chapter 15 is at the very core of this book. It covers the ways in which the computer can help our businesses with the conversion and manipulation of data into information. Finally, in Chapter 16 we describe some of those areas where the computer is actually programmed to control operational applications.

14

Introduction to Information Technology

Introduction

Information technology sounds a rather grand term but what does it actually mean? We understand it to mean the storage, manipulation and/or transmission of data using computers. In this chapter we introduce you to what a computer (the hardware) is, and what happens with all the equipment that comes with it (the peripherals), in such a way that you are not blinded by science. Hopefully, by the end of the chapter you will have a good understanding of the meaning of most of the current computer jargon.

What is a Computer?

If we are to make a case for computerization in the right circumstances we need to be certain we understand what we mean by *a computer*. This is not as straightforward as it may seem. The development of the silicon chip and the printed circuit have led to the miniaturization, and reduction in cost, of computer technology to the extent that there are small computers, for example, in our watches, controlling our central heating systems and even in children's toys. We do not intend to get too technical in answering our question *What is a computer?* but to look at it mainly in the context of what it can do for us in the work situation.

For our purposes we will regard the computer as basically a device for storing, analysing and comparing data, and for assisting in its transfer from one location to another. We will discuss these and other uses in detail later. To carry out these tasks the modern computer makes use of the ability of thin slivers of silicon (the CHIP) to have miniaturized electronic circuits etched on their

189

surface. These chips and their associated circuitry are known as microprocessors and they have the capacity to retain the data which is passed across them and to compare the stored data with new data which is fed to them. They have the ability to sort the data they are holding, for example, into date order, or into ascending or descending order of size. The storage capacity of the computer can be magnified many times over by the use of tape storage devices (rather like taped cassette music) or by the use of disks (rather like music stored on compact disk). We describe storage devices more fully on page 199.

The computer has a CENTRAL PROCESSOR UNIT (CPU) – the nerve centre which takes in instructions and data and performs the appropriate calculations. The size of the CPU is usually expressed in KILOBYTES (Kbytes or Kb) and denotes the amount of data or instructions it can hold. Eight BITS of data = 1 BYTE; 1024 (or 2^{10}) bytes = 1 kilobyte in the strange *binary* (i.e. based on 2) mathematical world of the computer expert. One byte of data can be used to hold an alphabetic character, a number, a punctuation mark or, on some machines, a code for determining the colours on the computer screen. The size of the CPU is important as it will have an effect on the types of *software* (programs) that can be run on it. The size of the computer *memory* is also important and we hear such expressions as *8-bit, 16-bit* and *32-bit* machines – this is an indication of how much data the chip can handle at one time and, therefore, an indication of how fast the computer might be able to handle our transactions.

In order to run programs and enter data into the computer there is a need for what are called INPUT DEVICES – a very common example of this is the keyboard. Similarly, there is a need to get information out in the form of reports, etc., and the mechanisms that provide for this are known as OUTPUT DEVICES – a common example of which is the printer. We will look at some of these input/output devices in more detail shortly but first we look at the different types of computer available.

Types of Computer

There are four main types of computer – the main-frame, mini-computer, microcomputer and personal computer (PC). The basic features are the same – a central processor where the calculations are carried out, some internal memory for holding data or text that has been worked on, extended memory for storage in the form of magnetic tapes and/or disks, and input/output devices. The essential difference between the four types is in the size of their CPU and memory storage, with the main-frame being largest of the four, the PC the smallest and the minicomputer and microcomputer being somewhere in between.

The advantages of larger CPUs are that greater volumes of data can be processed more quickly than on smaller processors and more complex programs can be run on them. The disadvantages of the main-frame with its large CPU lie not only in the high initial financial outlay on the hardware but also on the cost of adaptation of the premises to give the main-frame its essential dust-free, temperature-controlled environment in which to operate. The financial factor is also felt in terms of the software, which is generally more expensive than that produced to run on their smaller but more numerous relatives, the mini, the micro and the PC.

The main advantage of the mini and the micro is that they do not require a special environment in which to operate. When you add to that the fact that they are usually cheaper to purchase than a main-frame you will see that the installation/set up costs can be significantly lower than those for a main-frame. However, the mini/microcomputers can be handicapped by the lack of size of their CPUs, when compared with the main-frame. Both the main-frame and the mini/microcomputers have the facility to run extra TERMINALS or WORK STATIONS from them, making it possible for several operators to have access to the data at the same time. The larger the CPU, the more terminals the computer can support without an unacceptable reduction in the time taken to process commands or data. So far as differences between the microcomputer and the minicomputer are concerned, there is little for the *amateur* to choose between them. In very general terms a microcomputer can support a network (see page 199) of up to about twenty SCREENS or SLAVE STATIONS, whereas the larger minicomputer can support up to about three times as many.

The main advantage of the PC (see Figure 14.1) over its bigger brothers is its low cost. Good PC hardware can be purchased for less than £1,000 at the time of writing. Even the addition of a colour facility, HARD DISKS for additional storage capacity and a good quality printer will only set your bank account back by about £1,500. Although PCs can be networked together, this ability is severely limited when compared to the mini, micro and mainframe. Also, when compared to the larger types of computer, the PC can be very slow to process data and instructions and can only cope with relatively low volumes of data. However, in many business situations the speed and capacity of the PC may well be sufficient.

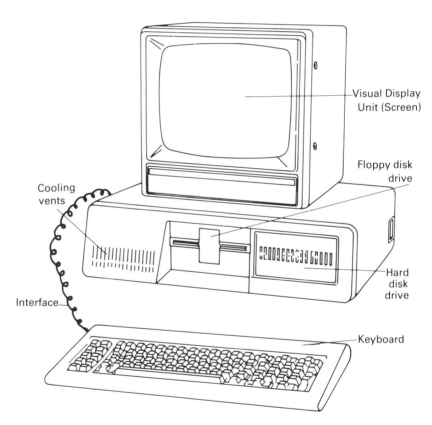

Figure 14.1
The Personal Computer (PC)

Input Devices

It is not our intention to try and give a complete list of all the input devices currently available for getting data or text into the computer, but to cover some of the more common ones. They are:

a keyboards;
b punched cards/paper tape/magnetic tape;
c optical character readers;
d document scanners;
e document readers;
f bar code scanners;
g smart cards and swipe cards;
h light pens;
i the mouse;
j voice.

Keyboard. The KEYBOARD is probably the most obvious and frequently used input device. Copied from the traditional Qwerty typewriter keyboard, it has additional keys to allow for specific computer control functions. With some computer packages it is possible to program certain keys to carry out a series of commands connected with routine, pre-planned operations which the computer then processes automatically.

Punched Cards/Paper Tape/Magnetic Tape. Quite early in the development of computers it was recognized that inputting data directly into a computer via a keyboard was very slow when compared with the ability of the computer to receive and process vast quantities of data very quickly. To cope with this, if the data could not be captured at source, for example by the modern supermarket till, it would be prepared for inputting OFF-LINE, that is, the keyboard was not connected directly to the computer. The key impressions would record the data onto an intermediate medium, originally by cutting holes in cards (known as PUNCHED CARDS) coded into appropriate patterns, and the codes would be read by shining light through the coded holes. An alternative to the punched card was perforated paper tape, and this was superseded by magnetic tape for fast inputting. Off-line inputting, while not affecting the speed of operation at the keyboard, at least does not tie up the computer for long periods of slow data input as it separates the input function from the process function.

Optical Character Readers. Another development was the design of a reader for OPTICAL CHARACTER RECOGNITION (OCR). These optical characters are almost identical to ordinary alphabetic/numeric characters and so could be read by the human eye *and* the computer. An example is the number on the bottom of our cheques which allows the bank to identify our account number. OCRs provide the means whereby the normal alphabetic letters and numbers are slightly altered (to fit within a unique grid) so that when they are *read* by the optical reader, each character produces a unique signal to be read into the computer.

Document Scanners. An alternative to optical character recognition, and a forerunner of the document reader which is discussed next, is the DOCUMENT SCANNER. This device is much used by census takers who require the person completing the questionnaire to fill in various boxes on a form. For example, when requiring details of the respondent's age there will probably be a series of boxes to indicate the range in which the age actually falls. When the form is scanned by the document scanner it notes which boxes are marked and adds up all those in each age range. In this way a very quick and perfectly accurate sum of each category is instantly available for statistical analysis.

Document Readers. One of the drawbacks to computerized information systems or electronic mail systems has been the need to type into the computer through the keyboard any document that has been received as HARD COPY. Hard copy distinguishes paper-based documents from those documents held or filed on the computer electronically. Often the text on the hard copy is in a form which can be used directly by the computer so this typing chore is really quite wasteful of the time of the typist or keyboard operator. Fortunately, there are now devices on the market such as the DOCUMENT READER which will read ordinary typewritten text on a document and convert it into electronic impulses for storage on the computer. This is a distinct step forward from the older technology of optical character recognition. As yet, these document readers are very expensive but this is likely to change as the technology improves. Even now, the developments in FACSIMILE (or FAX) technology are progressing so quickly that most offices will soon have them available. The FAX machine reads a document (or drawing) and converts the image to electrical impulses for transmission (via the telephone) to another FAX machine. Hence a document can be copied across from one location to another (thousands of miles apart) almost instantaneously. This is a real boon where the quick transfer of information is important. The technology is already available whereby FAXs can be received directly into our computers.

Bar Code Scanners. One input device which is gaining tremendous popularity in the retail trade is the BAR CODE SCANNER which automatically reads the bar codes on the side of goods as they are passed over the scanner by the checkout operator. With this device, at the same time as the bill is prepared for the individual customer, it is aggregated to the store total for the day and, at the end of the day, the store's total will be added to the totals from other stores in the chain to give an immediate complete record of the day's takings. A double benefit is that each transaction is recorded automatically for stock control purposes as well. Previously the till would have captured all this data but the bar code scanner removes the need for the operator to key in the data, thus improving speed and accuracy.

Smart and Swipe Cards. Other input devices used in the retail trade are those such as the SMART CARD, where credit is pre-purchased like the British Telecom Phonecard, which tells the retailer's computer how much credit we have. The SWIPE CARD is *wiped* through a reader and automatically deducts the value of the purchases from the customer's account and credits the value to the retailer's account.

Light Pens. Away from the retail trade and into the area of design and development there is a growing usage of the LIGHT PEN as an input device. The light pen is used as a pen actually to draw the image on the VDU (Visual Display Unit). The drawing can then be saved or manipulated along with any other material on the screen.

Mouse. We have described the keyboard as a computer input

device. It is also a *control* device for moving the CURSOR around the screen and inputting the commands such as *delete, file*, etc., which the computer needs in order to function. There is now a device available in many computer installations to augment the keyboard as a control device, and that is the MOUSE. In computer terms a mouse is a device which is connected to the computer and allows an arrow to be directed across the face of the VDU. By moving the mouse (a small box on a single castor) across the surface of the desk, the point of the arrow is directed across the VDU and onto a choice from a list or MENU displayed on the screen. When the button on top of the mouse is *clicked*, that choice is selected for input into the computer. In this way the mouse is both an input and control device.

Voice. As the technology develops, more and more input devices appear on the market. Voice input directly to computers has made great strides forward during the last few years but has a long way to go before it plays any large role in this field.

We have been able to cover only some of the most commonly used input devices in this section. When we come to discuss operational applications on the computer in Chapter 16 we shall briefly mention others, such as temperature sensors, but for the time being we will leave input devices and look at how we get material *out* of the computer.

Output Devices

As with input devices, there are many different output devices, each with their own specific characteristics and uses. We shall describe some of the output devices most frequently used in business computer applications. They are:

a   visual display units;
b   printers;
c   plotters;
d   voice output;
e   electro-mechanical;
f   modems.

Visual Display Units. Almost all computers have a visual display unit (VDU), looking rather like a television screen, as the principal output device. The screen records the instructions we are keying (or 'mousing') into the computer and relays back to us the commands that the computer is accepting. If we are using a mouse, then the VDU shows us where the mouse is situated ready for the *click* to bring the command or data into play. The VDU will also display the results of our analyses, tables, reports, etc.

Printers. Running close second to the VDU as the most frequently used output device is the PRINTER. The printer produces the *hard copy*, and these days comes in many forms and sizes. The main types of printer available to us in the early 1990s are the DAISYWHEEL, the DOT MATRIX, the LASER PRINTER, with the newer INK JET printers starting to appear. The daisywheel uses a spinning printer head with alphabetic and numeric characters, and punctuation marks. The dot matrix functions by forming the characters out of dots. The other differences between the daisy wheel and the dot matrix printers are that the daisy wheel is slower and, in general, noisier than the dot matrix but the quality of its print is much clearer than that of the dot matrix. This is a generalization, of course, and like most generalizations is open to some argument. Modern dot matrix printers can produce what is known as letter quality print but in order to do that they compromise on their speed by over-striking each character two or three times. The dot matrix also has the advantage that it can print graphics. In addition, developments in dot matrix technology have given us the *48-pin* machine which prints at higher density and quality than the bottom-of-the-range laser printers. Laser printers, as the name suggests, rely on laser technology to process the text or picture images and are generally very fast and give a high quality result. The more expensive dot matrix and the laser printers have the facility to print in colour with a very wide range of shades. The ink jet printer fires its ink at the paper where it adheres because of an electrostatic charge. The main advantage of the ink jet is that it is virtually silent, apart from the paper feed. The main disadvantage is that the final result looks like a photocopy.

Plotters. A variant on the printer as an output device is the PLOTTER. The principal advantage of the plotter is that it can produce very accurate diagrams and graphs, and some have the added advantage that they can produce these in colour.

Voice. As we mentioned earlier, many organizations are researching voice input devices but they have not yet made great advances, although some of the High Street banks hope to offer the voice input facility to their customers in the near future. However, there have been some developments in the use of the electronic voice device as an output route from the computer. One area in which this is currently available is in home banking systems. We telephone the bank's computer and give our account number (or its code) and a personal identification number via a small keyboard and the metallic, robot-like voice tells us how much cash we have in our account!

Electro-mechanical. We mentioned above that we would briefly be discussing sensors as input devices in Chapter 16. Well, an opposite action to the sensor is for the computer to make something happen by use of mechanical or electronic output. Perhaps one very good example of electro-mechanical output from a computer is when a sensor in an aircraft detects that the aircraft is diving or climbing, when it ought to be flying level. The computer passes instructions to the engine and control surfaces of the aeroplane, the elevators, to make adjustments so that the aircraft neither climbs nor descends.

Modems. Perhaps the device which is growing fastest in popularity as both an input and output device is the MODEM. The MOdulator/DEModulator converts text, data or images from our computer into electrical impulses for transmission down the telephone line to another computer installation, remote from our location. A similar modem converts the electrical impulses back into computer-recognizable messages for reuse on that remote computer. In this way the modem allows data and text (the so-called electronic mail) which has been input to a computer in a location remote from our machine to be brought into our computer for use. It also allows data or text which we have prepared on our installation to be output to another, remote computer.

Storage Devices

Yet another range of devices that could be considered as both input and output devices are the storage devices. As output devices they receive from the computer data, text or reports that are no longer required within the computer to be worked on. Rather than losing this data when the computer is switched off at the end of a shift, or losing it by overwriting it with the next set of data, there is a need to put it somewhere for safekeeping, storage or archiving. Storage can be on a variety of media but the most commonly used are:

a *Magnetic disk.* In FLOPPY form the magnetic disk is available to most PCs and is capable of storing the contents of the computer memory several times over. In hard disk form, either built into the computer or attached as a peripheral device, the magnetic disk will be able to store the contents of the computer to an even greater extent. These hard disks can have a capacity in excess of 500 times that of the floppy disks.

b *Magnetic tape.* Mainly used these days for backup purposes, that is, the storage of huge amounts of data from hard disks as a security process in case the main disk is damaged in some way or the data held on it is corrupted and becomes unusable.

In addition to being a storage device the DISK DRIVE can be one of the principal input devices, certainly so far as data or text prepared off-site or on another computer is concerned. The disk is simply inserted into the disk drive and when the appropriate commands are keyed in, the programs, data or text are entered into the computer's memory. Of course, the two computers have to be COMPATIBLE, that is, they both have to recognize the signals coming from and going to the disk as having the same meaning to both computers; they have to be in the same LANGUAGE to be understood, just as with the spoken word.

Networking

Mention has been made several times of the need and ability of several computers to link in and work together on corporate or centrally held data. One of the most powerful developments in the recent past has been the ability to link together mainframes, minis, micros and PCs. This NETWORKING makes it seem that every operator has access to the total database of information in the organization and to all the programs that are available on the central computer. It can also mean that it is possible for all computers on the network to communicate with each other. The implications of this are enormous. We computer users are at last set free (to some extent) of the central Computer Departments and *their* priorities. From a management information system point of view it means that the manager or professional can have his/her own reports from the central database, formatted in a way most suitable to themselves and at a time when they best need the information. This is a great improvement on the situation where we were beholden to the Computer Department and their efforts to satisfy our information needs!

These linkings of computers can be on a local area network (LAN), that is, usually within the same building, or on a wide area network (WAN), across to other buildings (see Figure 14.2). Wide area networks can be unlimited by distance and are often hundreds of miles apart. From a business point of view, no longer do all our staff need to be in corporate headquarters to participate in the MIS. It also makes easier the concept of working from home as, with our home computer, we could still have access to the management information system. Arguments over centralization or decentralization no longer have the power of previous decades. No longer do all the financial institutions have to cluster in the Square Mile (City of London) to participate at the centre of financial power. This is not to say that they will not continue to do so but for reasons other than electronic information flow!

The Computer and Security

Information flows between managers and professionals, between headquarters and decentralized operations, between service provider and customer can be the life blood of the business. It is particularly worrying, therefore, to hear of breakdowns in security surrounding computers and databases. Indeed, the very developments (modems, LANs, WANs, etc.) which we have been praising so highly not only open up our corporate information systems to

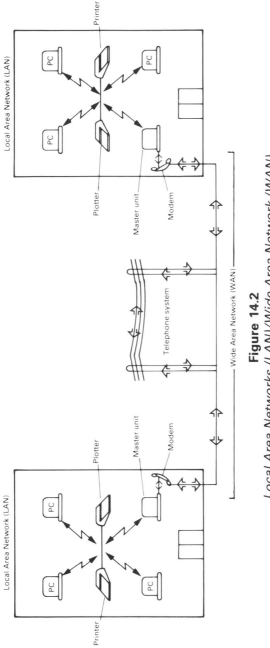

Figure 14.2
Local Area Networks (LAN)/Wide Area Network (WAN)

our own authorized users but also, by their very nature, to unauthorized users as well. The term HACKER, to mean some unauthorized person who interrogates someone else's computer or database to steal, read, corrupt or destroy the data held therein, has come into almost everyday speech. A new crime nowadays is *hacker blackmail* whereby data is corrupted and money has to change hands before the hacker will fix it. This type of crime would appear to be particularly popular in Italy where it has become known as *data kidnapping*. It seems that with the ever growing opportunities to input to, or receive output from, computers come the growing opportunities for improper use. So what can we do about this modern phenomenon?

Well, the first thing we might do is to institute a system of passwords, which allow authorized people to gain access to the computer and its contents or at least to their part of the computer and its contents. Passwords can be of varying power, so that only certain people have access to certain data, for example, only the most trusted or senior employees could have access to the most sensitive data. Passwords can also restrict users only to read the data and not to alter it or take copies. You will see straight away how this could hinder the unauthorized use of data, so long as the hackers do not find out the particular code or password.

Another aspect of security concerns the obligations placed on us by the Data Protection Act 1984. The Act requires computer users to ensure that the data they hold on living individuals is both accurate and secure. All of us will be aware of how easy or difficult it is in our organizations to obtain personal information on colleagues or customers from the *paper* files without authorization. Often it is only the sheer volume of files that makes it impossible for us easily and quickly to steal large amounts of such data. For a long time, as the majority of the working population was computer illiterate, the mere fact that information was held on the computer was almost sufficient security in itself. Now, with the arrival of the computer on almost every desk and our ready encouragement to employees to become computer literate, we can no longer be sure that the computerized systems are secure. We must design into our management information systems sufficient safeguards to protect the integrity of the database and the programs that run it from unauthorized use.

Finally, one aspect of security that has recently received considerable publicity is the business of the so-called COMPUTER VIRUSES. It would seem that some clever programmers have designed programs that *invade* our computer systems and have the ability to hide in our own programs and/or databases to be recalled into action automatically, perhaps on a particular date (for example, Friday 13th and 1 April are two of the dates sometimes chosen). When they are activated they can corrupt the data and/or the programs and display some unusual graphics on the VDU (for example, a bouncing ball and tumbling characters are popular displays).

So, what can we do if our computer systems are *infected* by one of these viruses? One option is to re-format our hard disk and start all over again making sure that we do not use any programs or data that have been transferred from our hard disk. This is a slow and tedious business as it can mean re-constituting the databases from scratch. There is no guarantee that this will work as some viruses hide themselves so well on the disk that a re-format leaves them unaffected. In fact, they are specifically designed to protect themselves by rejecting the reformat in their SECTOR.

Another option, in parallel with the approach to viruses in humans, is to *inoculate* against them. However, unlike humans, computers can only be inoculated after the virus has struck and the machine is infected. What the inoculation does is to encapsulate the virus in computer code, working rather like a white blood cell eating a virus and therefore making it harmless. With this method the computer virus is not destroyed but is rendered harmless, or so we think. The only way to be really sure that we do not still have a virus working like a time bomb after infection is to scrap the hard disk completely and replace it with a new one. However, perhaps before taking such drastic action we might seek the help of a specialist who is able to diagnose the problem and recommend some appropriate action.

Perhaps the best protection against the infection of our computers by viruses is always to check against a *virus checker* every disk that is going to be used. This would be a defence against all viruses known or thought to be known to mankind. The problem is that new mutations can be developed which might not be recognized as a virus by the checker and so could possibly sneak past our defences.

An alternative to this is always to use new software and avoid *borrowed* copies of programs and never, never allow anyone to bring in copies of games or their own software to use on the business's computers.

Conclusion

In this chapter we have tried to cover what a computer is and what a computer, and its peripherals, does for us. We have compared the various types of computer that are available to us and looked at the linking of computers together in networks. Finally, we looked at computer security and the worrying topics of hackers and computer viruses. In the next chapter we bring together the subjects of management information systems and information technology.

15

Management Information and the Computer

Introduction

In the previous chapter we looked generally at what a computer is and does. In this chapter we shall examine some of the ways the computer can help in the business world. We shall look at the principal types of application on the computer, particularly so far as they have a contribution to make to management information. We shall concentrate first on the basic management information system, looking at manual systems and answering the question of 'Why computerize?' We move on to discuss databases, as these are the main component of modern management information systems. Then we look at text/word processing and spreadsheets. After that we shall spend a little time on accountancy systems as the generator of management information and then discuss the use of statistics packages on the computer. Next, we look briefly at database marketing and the application of expert systems before ending with sections on project planning and simulation/modelling.

Manual Management Information Systems

Organizations are usually set up to do something such as manufacture, sell, repair, move/remove, store, break up, dispose of, etc., materials or to provide services, for example, legal, advertising, health, etc. Very rarely are organizations set up to gather, store, retrieve, analyse and distribute information, although this does happen in some cases. Usually the operating side of the business is set up according to certain basic principles or legal requirements and the initial management information systems tend to be fairly rudimentary. For those organizations which are set up with the purpose of making a profit, information systems at the outset tend to focus on what has been bought (and therefore to whom we owe money), on the costs of manufacture or adaptation, on the costs of storage and distribution, and on sales (and therefore, who owes us money). To cope with these information needs we keep records of what we buy at what cost, and from whom, and to whom we sell our goods and services, and at what price. We keep other information for specific reasons and for statutory purposes such as Value Added Tax, Income Tax, Corporation Tax, etc.

In the initial stages of an organization's life we tend not to need information systems for the purpose of management decision making, such as our pricing policy. It would probably just be a question of testing what the market will stand in terms of price and, in any case, we can remember what happened last time. Our memory usually serves us well in this situation because there are such small amounts of information available. However, it is not long before we and/or the management want to know how much we paid for a particular raw material, what it cost us to turn it into our finished product, what we sold it for and in what volumes – in order to decide such things as:

- whether to negotiate a different buying price for raw materials;
- whether to change our supplier;
- whether to improve our methods of manufacturing and pro-ductivity;
- whether we can improve our marketing and distribution;
- whether we can/should revise our sales price.

Where the quantity of data is relatively small and there is little sorting and re-sorting of the individual records into different categories required, and/or infrequent need to update the data, there is little need for computerization. A manual system is readily understood by the owner/manager and s/he can see at a glance what is happening in the business. A good card index of customers or clients will easily keep track of their addresses and contact dates. A good set of simple ledgers will keep track of purchases and sales and, at the same time, provide the basis for keeping records for taxation and other statutory purposes. One principle advantage of manual systems is that they are always available, whatever else is happening in the business and other systems being worked on, and they do not break down! One disadvantage of small computer systems is that there is a strong possibility that the application running at a particular time is not the one you actually need at that moment. This is because the routine applications such as payroll and invoicing usually have to be carried out according to systematic office procedures. This need for routine can make random access to the small computer installation both inefficient and inconvenient when compared with the ready availability of material in the manual systems. Also, and perhaps most important of all, computer systems and their associated peripheral devices cost money which may well be better invested in the directly productive areas at the time of business start up.

All of the above reasons might be sufficient in themselves for leading to a decision not to computerize. However, perhaps one of the greatest obstacles to computerization for the person without computer skills is the bewildering plethora of different computer systems on sale and the totally incomprehensible jargon talked by the computer experts, as you will now know. At a time when the new entrepreneur is grappling with the problems of setting up the new business, coping with all the production, legal and financial problems, the very last skill that s/he feels capable of developing is the skill of being his/her own computer expert.

Why Computerize?

So, why computerize if there are so many convincing reasons against it? Perhaps the simplest answer to this question is that all the above arguments against computerization can be overcome, albeit some more easily than others, and there can be enormous advantages resulting from computerization. Let us look at both some of the benefits of computerization and some of the difficulties that manual systems present.

One important issue is the volume of records and data held within the organization and the requirement regularly to sort and/or update the data. Anyone in even the smallest business knows that the organization has only to survive and continue operating for as little as a year and the volume of records and data can grow to alarming proportions. Even a modest computer system can cope with substantial volumes of data that would otherwise be contained in large quantities of paper records. When the volume of paper gets too great, then the problems of remembering where particular records are filed, retrieving them readily and being able easily to amend or update them quickly becomes almost insurmountable.

Another good reason for computerization is that copies, known as *backup* copies, of the data can be made electronically and stored remotely from the source, thus making them secure from loss due to fire, or other damage in the office where they would normally be stored and used. Another security aspect is confidentiality, in that there can be systems of electronic as well as physical barriers to prevent unauthorized access to the commercial secrets of the organization. This makes, with certain safeguards, the data held on computer more secure than that in paper files where physical security is usually the only barrier to improper use.

The question of the cost of equipment as a barrier to computerization is becoming less valid by the day. The cost of the computer equipment – the computer itself, visual display units, printers, etc. – is coming down all the time and in the early 1990s small computer systems can be bought for little more than the price of an electric typewriter. They need no special environment in which to work and run off the normal power supplies. The software – that is the computer programs – that run on them are becoming more and more readily available in tried and tested PACKAGES at relatively low cost and presented in USER-FRIENDLY ways. By packages we mean a complete computer system which is bought to do a pre-defined job such as payroll in its entirety. By user-friendly we mean capable of being used by the lay person rather than being the province only of the computer expert. Little or no re-programming is required, the packages are simply installed on the machine and operated in a TURN-KEY fashion, that is, they are started rather like starting your family car – you simply put the key into the ignition and turn it. The engine starts and you drive away. You do not need training nor qualifications in motor engineering to get underway in your car, though you do need to be able to drive of course. Computer turn-key systems are just as straightforward as starting your car.

Let us address the question of the lack of computer expertise as a barrier to computerization. We have answered this in part in the paragraph above, in terms of the development of user-friendly, turn-key computer packages. The big advantage of these packages is that they require no programming ability on the part of the operator to get them working. The only training needed is to learn the operation of the computer and then the operation of the computer packages you intend to use. These days most computers have relatively clear manuals for their use and where this is not so, a ready cottage industry seems to have grown up to write clear training manuals for the un-enlightened. The same applies to the software. Most program writers these days have learnt that it is virtually impossible to sell their product if it is not supported by clear instructions for its use and even the provision of good practice exercises. As a result of these developments, the barrier of lack of computer expertise as the reason for not computerizing our business operations has become considerably less valid.

Finally, the problem of computer availability can be overcome by networking two or more computers, linked to the same store of programs and data (as we explained on page 200). This will allow two or more operators to access these programs and data simultaneously.

So, we have seen that there are some good reasons why we might computerize. However, each case needs to be looked at on its merits; computerization is not a universal panacea for all situations.

Databases

As we discussed earlier in this chapter, before the advent of computers, those organizations which required information on customers, suppliers, etc., tended to use card index systems to hold the data. These systems were very good but required considerable clerical work to keep them up to date. It was also a slow process to get at the data and convert it manually into the information which we needed – an obvious case for computerization. So, in the early days of computing, databases were largely electronic card index systems. They made life considerably easier for the holder of large volumes of data on clients, customers, spare parts, etc., which were subject to regular amendment and updating. For example, staff records or customer information might be filed by surname in alphabetic order, or by salary record number or customer number, or by some sort of code to indicate department, location, etc. The possession of part of the identifying information, that is, either the surname when the records were filed in numerical order, or the customer invoice number when the records were filed in alphabetical order, used to make life difficult if not impossible when the computer operator could not re-sort the records into the required order.

However, all was not perfect, even with this ability to update the records, sort and re-sort them, and to print out the records or parts of the records selectively. The main problem was that the records could only be sorted or accessed according to the actual FILE (the unique storage area for data) they were held in and usually without reference to information held in other files. For example, details about an employee might be spread across several files – pay on the Payroll File, ages and length of service in the Pension File, etc. Where particular applications or management reports made it necessary to relate together the data, for example about one person, held in different files, it was usually necessary to amend the details of that person on every file in the system whenever a single piece of data changed. Without doubt this was a tedious and often long-winded process and frequently would be the cause of the information system falling into disrepute as no-one could guarantee that all the files were accurate. We mentioned earlier (page 202) that the Data Protection Act 1984 places a legal obligation upon computer users to ensure that the data they hold on living individuals is accurate. Where it is not, the individual can seek damages through the courts for any damage or distress caused by the inaccuracies and apply to the courts for rectification or erasure of the inaccurate data.

Also, with the early systems it was necessary to be very specific about the reports that were to be output from the database and obtain the help of the systems designer and/or programmers to design these reports. Because of this, any changes of mind by the manager requiring information out of *his/her* database necessitated reprogramming to obtain the new report or the new report format. This was often a long and costly business and not one beloved by computer programmers and systems analysts who would much rather be developing new applications than maintaining old ones. Fortunately, developments in computer technology have come to our rescue in two ways. First, the development of APPLICATION

SYSTEMS GENERATORS has led to the ability of non-computer people to design and re-design their own reports from their database systems. With these systems, the manager or computer user works through the procedure required to analyse the data and sets out the form of report wanted as output. Using the applications systems generator, the new routine is memorized for use in the future with the minimum of keying operations by the user. Our experience with these systems is that one needs only a minimum amount of computer knowledge to operate and amend these databases.

The second development is in the field of what are called RELATIONSHIP DATABASES. These are separate files in a database which might each contain data on a particular subject or person. When using the database, the computer automatically interrogates each of the files for the relevant data, using what is appropriate for the particular application in which the manager is interested. One very valuable characteristic of such systems is the ability to amend, delete or add to each item of data by inputting the amendment only once for it to be automatically altered in all the files.

Our new databases, therefore, are capable of easy amendment, capable of being used by *lay* professionals and managers with minimum intervention from the computer expert and, through the use of networks (both LANs and WANs), are available to all users at most times of the day. With the use of modems, we can escape from the physical boundaries of our office buildings and access the data from other sites by telephone. Developments in communication technology by the use of optical fibres and satellites have made worldwide access to these databases a practical proposition.

By such devices our management information systems have really come of age and we now look at some of the other practical applications on the computer and the ways in which they can help satisfy our information needs.

Word/Text Processing

Most people tend to use the expression WORD PROCESSING to mean the typing of words and figures into a computer or DEDICATED word processor. By *dedicated* we mean a piece of equipment which is designed and used solely for one purpose, in this case word processing, rather than having the ability to be used for other functions such as statistical or accountancy packages. There are developments taking place such as desktop publishing (DTP), about which we will say more later, which make the expression TEXT PROCESSING more appropriate – so this is the term we will use in this book. With the ready availability of computers to most managers there is an increasing incidence of managers developing typing/keyboard skills – which is particularly appropriate with the coming of electronic mail.

Typing into the computer via the *qwerty keyboard* is still the principal method of creating text on the computer although there are others (see pages 193–6) in lesser use. All modern text processing packages (whether running on dedicated word processors or on a computer) have the ability to store, amend and rearrange text, and recall it into use as required. Most are supported by 'spelling checkers' which will give us the choice to ensure correct spelling in English English or American English! As we rush towards the year 1992 and a single consumer market in Europe it is interesting to note the availability, or rather the lack of it, of accented characters, for example é (acute) or è (grave) in the French language, in text processing packages. Fortunately, some do allow us to re-define our keyboard to enable rarely used keys to take on this foreign function – all we need then is a daisy wheel containing the appropriate characters or their recognition by our dot matrix and laser printers. Some computers are already being programmed to perform as *translators* into different languages and operate, for example, like English/French and French/English dictionaries.

One important development has given us the ability to integrate our database with the text processing system. This allows us to transfer management information reports from our database into our text processing without retyping, simply by *importing* the report so that it appears as though it is typed as an integral part of our new document. This can be particularly useful if we are writing a report and wish to include some tables from our management information system.

The other development, already mentioned, which has received a considerable amount of publicity in the computer press, is DESKTOP PUBLISHING (DTP). With DTP, the text can not only be manipulated, as described above, but can also be physically squeezed or stretched to fit into columns of differing width or length. In addition, with these systems, diagrams, pictures and even photographs can now be included in the most appropriate place on the page with the text fitting around them. In parallel with these developments have come developments in printing technology. The laser printer makes it possible to output the hard copy from DTP systems extremely quickly and with very high quality images. As a result, it is now possible for managers to prepare their reports in a form that allows them to be directly typeset for printing without going through any intermediate process.

Spreadsheets

The SPREADSHEET has proved to be an absolute boon to the manager who needs to play *what if?* games – for example, what if the interest rate goes up by 1%, what if sales fall by 20% per annum or what if labour turnover increases by 10%? The spreadsheet allows us to set out a series of relationships and calculations which are then manipulated to see the effect of different assumptions. The spreadsheet is often used to work out the organization's future cash flow over a period of time, taking into account all the outgoings as well as all the incomes. Then, by inputting actual income and expenditure into the forecast cash flow and, using the spreadsheet to re-calculate month by month, we can see how variations from budget will affect profits at the end of the year.

The spreadsheet is a large matrix made up of a series of boxes, called cells, across the length and breadth of its surface (see Figure 15.1). The cells are arranged in rows and columns and may contain numbers or text. Numbers can be in the form of *values* or *formulae*, cells containing text are known as *labels*. By convention, the columns are named by alphabetic characters and the rows by numbers. This makes the name of the cell at the top left-hand side of the spreadsheet cell A1. The cell immediately to its right is cell B1, and the cell immediately beneath cell A1 is cell A2, and so on for as many columns and rows as the spreadsheet contains. The numerical values in the cells can be added to, subtracted from, multiplied or divided by, or indeed processed by any and every mathematical function. Similarly all the cells can be combined

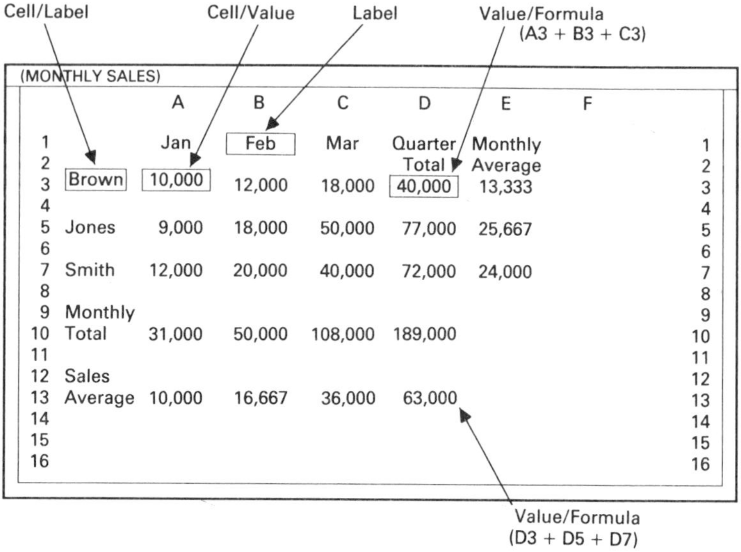

Figure 15.1
Sample Display of Spreadsheet

with all others in their row or column, and whole rows and columns can be manipulated.

The spreadsheet can be recalculated every time a value is changed in a cell, although this can be very time wasting if there are several changes to make at any time. Because of this, most spreadsheets have the facility to recalculate either automatically, after every cell is changed, or manually, at the end of making all our changes. Again, as with the database, most spreadsheets have the ability to produce reports and export them to a text processing system for incorporation into management reports.

Accounting Packages

It is not the purpose of this book to go into the subject of accounting systems. However, from a computing point of view they cannot be ignored as accounting routines were among the first to be computerized and have continued to play an important part in the finance functions of both public and private sector organizations. It is not surprising that this should be so. The very strengths of the computer lie in its ability to follow instructions to the letter and be completely accurate in doing any mathematical calculations. This is precisely the quality that the accountants need for their systems. What they need in addition is the ability to input a particular item, say of expenditure, only once and for the computer then to *post* it to the various ledgers for the different accountancy purposes, for example VAT returns, cash flow, profit-and-loss account, etc. One word of warning, however: some accountancy knowledge is needed to use successfully most of the accountancy packages.

From a management information point of view this ability to update financial records constantly and immediately means that financial information should be available almost on tap, to be drawn on whenever the manager needs it. Most computerized financial systems record all financial transactions in an orderly way so as to analyse them on a regular basis and produce routine reports, such as outstanding invoices over the accounting period. In addition, they often combine some of the features of databases and spreadsheets and, where they have graphics packages incorporated into their design, can produce graphical or pictorial representations of the accounts month by month. As well as the routine reports, most accounts packages have the ability to produce request reports at any stage during the accounting year.

Finally, one of the computer's other strengths, the ability easily to make copies of the data held in its files, means that security copies of the whole organization's financial routines can and should be taken and stored in a fireproof safe or remote from the site in case of fire. This is an invaluable feature as most organizations would go out of business if they lost all their financial records and had no means of reconstituting them.

Statistics Packages

This book would be incomplete if no mention was made of the statistics packages that are available today. Off-the-shelf packages allow us to do all those troublesome calculations that appear in Part 2 of this book, ranging from calculating averages to hypothesis testing and multiple regression. Only a little statistical knowledge is needed to use the statistical packages but quite a lot of statistical knowledge is usually needed to *interpret* the results they produce. However, the same qualities that make the accounts packages so valuable to the accountant – the ability to follow rules and to be totally accurate in one's mathematical calculations – make the statistics packages a boon to the statistician. This is particularly the case when handling large amounts of data. Before these packages became available, the statistician had to rely on the computer expert to set up and operate the statistical techniques on the computer, often a time-consuming and frustrating exercise. Now, manager/statisticians can do it themselves, with the flexibility to re-test/re-run the calculations to their hearts' content!

Database Marketing

One of the great attractions of computer systems is their versatility and few applications demonstrate this better than DATABASE MARKETING. As the name suggests we make use of our computerized database and we combine it with our text processing system to help us in our marketing operation. Most text processors available today have the facility to MAILMERGE. By this we mean the facility to merge a standard letter with a list of names and addresses. A standard letter might be prepared, say, for a marketing shot to our customers. The letter might describe a new product or a new service. We could then go to our database and screen the total list of customers or clients to select those most likely to respond to our letter. We would then use the *mailmerge* facility to print and send out letters to those selected customers.

Let's take an example. Suppose the marketing professional wants to target potential customers below the age of thirty, who live in a particular television region and who have previously bought electronic equipment from the company since the beginning of 1988. The screening, or filtering (as it is sometimes called), of the data against these criteria would be done by instructing the computer to find all the people on the database who matched the criteria:

$$age = <30;$$
$$TV = Thames;$$
$$year = >1987.$$

In this way, the records of the selected customers would be called up from the database and all that is needed to send each of them a personalized top copy of our standard letter is to mailmerge their addresses with it. If used in this way, database marketing can be very cost effective when compared with the cost of mailshots to all our customers regardless of their potential – the number of letters sent is much reduced and the likely response is greater because we have been able to be selective.

Although we have used database marketing with a targeted mail shot as our example to explain the selective filtering ability of the computer, the principles involved are of tremendous value in many different business situations. Another good example could be preventive maintenance of machinery on customers' premises. As before, the computer operator would decide what criteria were important in the selections – in this case, all the items of machinery located in a particular area which had not been serviced within the past eleven months. The computer, merging its filtered database and its text processing systems, would send out letters telling the customers of the intention of an engineer to visit them to service the machines on a particular day.

Integrated Packages

Some of the computer systems which make things even easier for us are those called INTEGRATED PACKAGES. With integrated packages the programmers have combined the various individual programs we need together so that the database, word processing, spread-sheet and modem communications software are all included in the same SHELL, making the transfer of data or text between them extremely simple.

Expert Systems

Computers have been described somewhat extravagantly by some writers as having *artificial intelligence*. The EXPERT SYSTEM is the closest development yet to artificial intelligence. In the late 1980s, developments in computer hardware and software have made the concept of expert systems generally available to anyone with a respectable personal computer, that is, one with a decent size of CPU internal memory and hard disk external storage.

The expert system brings together, in a computer, a knowledge base in a particular field and the rules by which a human expert in that field might arrive at a decision. The system will probably never completely replace the experts but will make their knowledge, and their skill in applying that knowledge, available widely in the organization. It should also ensure their time is used more effectively by avoiding the need for them to be involved in the minutiae of all mundane decisions.

The biggest benefit of these expert systems is that the knowledge bases and the rules are constructed using readable English which is simple to learn and use, thus allowing the essential active participation of the business specialist in the creation of their expert system. The knowledge base is a combination of the database and the record of the data entered in the current session together with conclusions arrived at – with the process *learnt* by the computer as it goes along. The rules are usually associated with questions which guide the user through the consultation with the expert system and follow the classic *if . . . then . . .* (Boolean) format. For example, a meteorological expert system might have the rules:

If atmospheric pressure is above 1020 millibars and steady or rising,
Then settled weather is likely to follow.

If Dickens' Mr Micawber had an expert system, it might have the rules:

If annual income twenty pounds,
and annual expenditure nineteen nineteen six,
Then result happiness.
If annual income twenty pounds,
and annual expenditure twenty pounds nought and six,
Then result misery.

The main purpose of the expert system is to help managers and professionals make their decisions and there are two broad categories of expert systems to assist in this:

a   Advisory systems, in which the expert's knowledge can be made available to advise within a specific context. An example is in the field of employment legislation where one of the expert packages available allows the user to interrogate it on specific problems. For example, by inputting the details of the specific disciplinary situation, the computer will provide advice and recommend an appropriate line of action to take. The system can also be required to explain why this advice was proffered and to re-evaluate it after inputting slightly different details of the problem to see how *robust* is the recommendation.

b   Knowledge communication, that is, providing less experienced people with the expertise of the expert. One good example of this could be where a large computer has broken down and the maintenance engineer on site could not possibly be expected to have the total knowledge to solve the problem. By connecting up to the manufacturer's expert system via a modem and telephone line, the maintenance engineer is given access to the total knowledge of the systems designers and to all other cases of similar symptoms. By knowing that it is a fault in the XYZ component, the engineer will know whether it is feasible to repair or replace that component. The expert system and the communications devices will have helped provide the essential knowledge without actually calling out the expert.

The range of applications for expert systems is limitless. One can imagine their use in such areas as actuarial work. An application in the field of employment law has already been mentioned and there are many other legal packages. Purchasing professionals could build into their systems their knowledge of quantity discounts, delivery times, quality tolerances and ranges of product specifications, alongside details of the known capabilities of different suppliers and the rules of the organization for assessing competitive tenders. The personnel professionals have their expert systems with integrated packages to help in organization charting, job evaluation, manpower planning and in recruitment where the database of candidates is matched against the specification of the vacancy. In the medical field we understand that an illness diagnostic expert system has been running at King's College Hospital in London for several years. The possibilities in finance and administration are endless.

Project Planning

Managers in all professions will have projects to oversee from time to time. Indeed, some managers will find that most of their work involves managing projects. Production engineers in particular will find this is so when they are designing, commissioning and bringing into action new plant and factories. Top levels of management will find that they are regularly presented with the task of co-ordinating projects spanning their whole organization. The development of computerized project management tools has already reached a level of sophistication whereby even fairly modest projects will benefit from their use, especially those where time, money and resources are short. (Are there any other types of project, you may well ask?) More importantly, computers allow us to manage complex projects far more easily than by using manual systems.

Most of the current batch of project planning systems are based on NETWORK ANALYSIS of which possibly the most familiar is the PERT (Programme Evaluation and Review Technique) programme which was developed by the US Navy in 1958. The use of the technique apparently saved two years from the construction and development stage of the Polaris submarine programme. Network analysis is a means of representing a project by an arrow diagram. Here, the sequence of arrows indicates the sequence of activities in the project and their dependence on other activities. Activities have a time for completion and events are the instantaneous points in time at which activities start or finish. The activities and events make up the network. The project planner works out the times of all the paths through the network and establishes the one taking the longest time. This is known as the CRITICAL PATH – *critical*, because any delay in this path will delay the overall project. The implications of this for managers is that they can concentrate their attention on those activities on the critical path, delegating other activities or giving them a lower priority. We explained in Chapter 1 how important it is for management information to be filtered so that managers are not overwhelmed by a mass of data. The identification of the critical path is an excellent example of this technique, allowing managers to concentrate their attention where it is needed most and to delegate less critical activities.

It is not the purpose of this book to describe network analysis in any detail and enthusiasts would be well advised to learn more about network analysis before trusting their projects to a computerized network system. However, while it is possible to plan simple small projects and manage them without the use of a computer, when the activities number several hundred or even several thousand, the computer becomes an essential tool. The computer not only helps us cope with the vast amounts of data but also allows us to make amendments to the network easily and get a rapid update of the management information from it. In addition, it is possible to plan resources – finance, plant and equipment, and people – using the network in order to get the optimum use from these resources. By inputting actual times of the completion of the activities into the computer it is possible to compare progress with plan, or to compare spending with budget, and finally to generate management information reports by which the project manager can control the project. The most modern of these packages make full use of the computer's availability to display different information at the same time, using sub-divisions of the VDU screen, or WINDOWS. The windows break up the screen to allow the project manager to continue looking at, say, the network while at the same time bringing cost information onto the screen.

Finally, as most modern project planning packages output the information that is needed, when it is needed and in a form that is suitable for its purpose (see page 3) we can see that these project planning packages are mini management information systems in themselves.

Mathematical Modelling

Most of us have heard about the use of physical models in business processes. Management services officers and others use models of factories and offices to enable them to design efficient layouts, aeronautical engineers use models of aeroplanes in a wind tunnel to give data on how the real aeroplane will fly, chemical engineers use models of chemical plants to try out their process before going to the expense of building the real thing. However, in addition to physical models there are MATHEMATICAL MODELS which are being used increasingly by managers and other professionals to help in their decision making. They use mathematical equations to model situations. The ability of computers to cope with thousands of mathematical calculations per minute has made it possible to model very complex situations and has extended the technique of modelling well beyond the realm of the mathematician. Because of this we now have available to us the means by which we can improve our decision making through mathematical modelling. Two well known examples of this type of model are:

a econometric models;
b financial models.

Econometric models. Econometric models are a set of mathematical equations which attempt to describe, or model, the economy. They try to set out the many complex relationships that exist within the economy. Econometric models are used by economists to test out different policy alternatives and to forecast the future economic situation based on different views or scenarios of the future. The techniques have been extended to other sectors of the economy and even to areas outside economics.

Financial models. Financial models represent the financial intricacies of an organization, showing what might happen to its finances against a range of different assumptions such as trading levels, interest rates, input costs and prices. A computerized spreadsheet (see page 213) is an application which represents a simple financial model of a part of an organization's finances, often the cash flow. The spreadsheet can also tell us, for example, what cash flows to expect at different levels of sales, or show what will happen to profit with changes in the price of raw materials.

Simulation

The last information application we wish to cover is that of SIMULATION. We discussed above the use of mathematical models to provide forecasts of dynamic, complex situations. The idea is to develop a set of equations describing how the information variables interact with each other. This technique is fine, so long as we know all the variables and are able to describe them mathematically. Much of the time our variables defy precise mathematical description and, even when we can so describe them, we cannot always represent their interaction with each other in mathematical terms. To get around these problems simulation techniques have been designed. These *simulate* the results or outcomes of operations that we are trying to model.

One of the most common simulation techniques, the MONTE CARLO method, relied in the past on the use of thrown dice (hence its name) to generate random quantities representing the incidence of certain events. Let us say, for example, that we are managing the refuelling of airliners at a major airport. The arrival intervals of the aeroplanes for refuelling and the volumes of fuel they require are the random variables. We can generate values of these variables for our simulation from the random number tables (see page 99) that are available.

Let us assume that our capacity to meet the refuelling needs of the aircraft depends on the availability of refuelling tankers, their capacity to carry fuel and the speed with which we can refill the tankers when they are emptied and get them back to their refuelling duties. In order to find the best combination of refuelling tankers to meet their task we can construct a model of the relationship between the constraints, for example, the rate of arrivals of the aircraft and the refuelling demands made upon the tankers. We can build into the model the capacities, etc., of the fuel tankers and, by throwing the dice time and time again and, by varying the constraints, find by trial and error which combination of tanker sizes and other factors produces the least delay in refuelling the aircraft. This is, at best, a very lengthy and frustrating process and could take days or weeks of constantly throwing the dice to get the optimum result. Our salvation is in the ability of the computer to allow us to design a model of the whole process, have programmed in a random number generator and ask it to simulate all the schedules and produce the optimum schedule to give the best fit within all the constraints.

Conclusion

In this all too brief look at information applications on the computer we are bound to have missed out some which you will think were worthy of inclusion. However, we have provided at least an introduction to this field where information technology can provide such a rich support to your management information and decision-making needs. In the following chapter we develop this theme further by looking at operational applications on the computer where, instead of providing information as the basis by which managers can intervene in the process, the computers themselves control the process with minimum human intervention.

16

Operational Applications on the Computer

Introduction

So far we have looked at the computer as a device for presenting managers with information to help them make their decisions. We want to spend a little time in this chapter looking at some applications where the computer actually makes the decisions itself according to rules that are programmed into it and based on data that is entered via sensors of some kind. We shall briefly describe such applications in areas as diverse as warehousing, production, computer-aided manufacturing and design, traffic control, environmental control and finance.

Warehousing

Computers have been used in stock control systems for many years. They have generated information, for example, on stock levels, economic re-order quantities, and have identified fast and slow moving stock lines. It is surprising, therefore, that the obvious extension into automated warehousing has been relatively slow and not kept pace with the developments in computer technology. There are, however, some good examples of the use of computers in retailing to control the storage, picking and assembly of items for despatch from the warehouse to the retail outlet.

In these situations, deliveries from suppliers to the warehouse are taken into a bulk storage area and sorted into units or pack sizes. These packs are of a size which experience has shown is the best for delivery to the shops. They are given their essential identifying information on arrival. They are then stored using automated conveyor belts or some other such system, and all the information on location and destination is recorded in the computer. As goods are sold from the retailer's shops, information is passed back to the warehouse and the computer starts to compile a list of replacement goods for subsequent picking and despatch to the shop. Goods in store are earmarked by the computer for these destinations and, when the time comes to assemble the load for delivery to the shop, the computer issues the instructions for these goods to be picked. The messages are sent from the computer either directly to gates holding back the products or to a robot picker which travels around the warehouse, reading the appropriate codes and picking the correct goods from the shelves. Finally the goods are transported to the assembly area where they are held in the delivery bays ready for loading onto the transporters for despatch to the appropriate shops.

Clearly the capital investment in such a system is enormous. However, picking from a warehouse has traditionally been a labour intensive activity and the pay-off comes from the reduction in the need to employ large numbers of manual or semi-skilled staff. In addition to this, it provides the ability to increase throughput by a considerable factor without any consequential need for an increase in the workforce. It is well known that, in the retail trade, a large percentage of business is done in the two or three months around Christmas. In order to cope with this massive fluctuation in throughput it would be necessary either to employ excessive numbers of under-used staff in the slack periods or to substantially increase the workforce during the busy period. The stability of employment in the automated warehouse when compared with the non-automated setup is a considerable additional benefit to the enterprise.

Last but not least, the computer ensures greater accuracy in the operation. No longer should a video be picked instead of a TV, or two of a four part set of furniture be sent on its way, or the newest rather than the oldest item selected. However, these types of computer system are best suited to products which come in uniform sizes, in relatively limited ranges. No retailer has, to our knowledge, successfully implemented a fully automated system which will cope with merchandise such as haberdashery stock which consists of thousands of different items or furniture which (unless it is flat packed) comes in such a variety of shapes and sizes.

Production Management

The type of technology used in the production process will dictate how the computer might help the Production Manager. Technology in this sense is intended to mean whether the process is continuous, batch or mass production.

In continuous production the computer could be invaluable in ensuring that the ingredients of the mixture are constantly adjusted to maintain the required specification. In batch production the computer can help by regulating the economic batch sizes and perhaps by ensuring that specific batches are channelled through individual machines to ensure even machine utilization. COMPUTER NUMERICAL CONTROL (CNC) has been developed to allow small batches to be produced economically where previously the extensive manual machine resetting made it uneconomic to produce small batches. With CNC, the computer *learns* from the operator the routine to follow in resetting the tools for the new batch. The process is considerably quicker and easier than manual resetting for each (minor) change in specification. The by-product of this production improvement is that the sales and marketing people can, at last, offer the customer the opportunity of purchasing his/her economic order quantity.

One area which has seen substantial development in the use of computers in the operational control of the process is the mass production of cars. These days it is unusual to see new car assembly lines designed to be manually operated. At last, robotics has taken over all those repetitive, boring car assembly line jobs that have been the focus of so much of our poor industrial relations over the years. In this area also, the use of the computer makes it economic to produce one-offs or small batches, in order to improve customer service without rendering production uneconomic.

Computer-aided Design and Manufacture

For many years the design of products, be they cars, buildings, ships, etc., has been carried out on the drawing board by draughtsmen/women. These skilled professionals have been responsible for translating ideas and specifications into working drawings, from which designs could be costed and then manufacturing could proceed. Any changes to the design due to cost, safety, environmental or other factors had to be laboriously changed by the draughtsman before it could be accurately re-costed and re-worked. Even in relatively simple manufacturing projects this could be a time wasting and costly process and it was not long before it was recognized that the computer could be an enormous help in this field. By the use of COMPUTER-AIDED DESIGN (CAD) the product can be designed to meet the specification exactly and to operate in its most efficient way. *What if* games can be played with alternative designs to see which is the most cost effective, or best meets other criteria, and the computer would then cost the final design automatically to the agreed specification.

In COMPUTER-AIDED MANUFACTURING (CAM), the processes and/or the machines involved in manufacturing are controlled by computers. Some of these installations are known as Computer Numerical Control (CNC) operations (see page 227) or COMPUTER PROCESS CONTROL operations (CPC). Where the same computer system controls both the CAD and the CAM operations, the whole system is known as COMPUTER-INTEGRATED MANUFACTURING (CIM).

Traffic Control

With the upsurge of the globe-trotting tourist and businessperson, the skies over our major cities have experienced greater and greater volumes of air traffic. The increase in the numbers of aeroplanes flying into and out of major airports has got to the stage where it is almost beyond the powers of mere human Air Traffic Controllers to cope with this gigantic game of three dimensional noughts and crosses. Instead, the air traffic data is fed into large computers from the aircraft's Flight Plan in order that the take-off and flight details produced ensure that each aircraft is maintained in its own unique air space, safely separated from all other aircraft.

Computers are also on board the modern aircraft, both civil and military. The civil aircraft will be *flown* by computer for substantial parts of its flight. The computer will be programmed to fly the aircraft at its allocated speed and altitude, and accurately on its designated airway. As the journey progresses and the aircraft burns up fuel it becomes lighter. As it becomes lighter it will seek to climb to a higher altitude unless something is done to compensate for the lighter weight. What happens is that the computer senses the changes and reduces engine power to maintain altitude. It also lowers the aircraft's nose in order to maintain speed at the lower power setting. In this way the on-board computer maintains the flight clearance allocated to the aircraft by the Air Traffic Controllers, or rather, by their computers!

In military aircraft, computer systems are responsible for identifying enemy aircraft from their *fingerprint* radar picture and controlling the firing mechanisms to shoot them down. The computers also guide pilotless aircraft and missiles onto their targets with a degree of accuracy that few pilots could achieve under the same circumstances.

It is not only the skies above our cities that are becoming overcrowded. We have only to try commuting to our offices in the major conurbations to recognize that road traffic in some of our cities is reaching almost crisis point. It may not be long before routes into and out of our cities are controlled by computers so that traffic flows are directed along routes that take them away from congested areas, rather than allowing the drivers to have the entire say as to their routes.

Already our rail traffic is controlled by computers which set lights at red, amber or green depending on what traffic or obstacles are ahead. The London Underground could not function at its current levels of activity and safety without the signalling system being managed by computers. As with air traffic, road and rail traffic has grown to a level where the direct input of the computer to control the traffic flow has become an absolute necessity if we are to travel safely and arrive reasonably on time.

Environmental Control

The computers in our aircraft not only control how the aircraft is flying or the delivery of weapons from a military aeroplane, but also such factors as the temperature and pressure in the aircraft cabin. In an industrial or commercial context this application can extend to control the whole environment in our offices, shops and factories. There are health and safety laws which regulate the temperature, etc., in our workplaces. These usually state, for example, that the temperature shall be maintained at a level which does not affect our health. Unfortunately, as we occupy our offices our body heat is transferred to the office. In addition to this, when we switch on our office equipment they emit heat to the environment as well. Sensors in modern offices detect these changes in temperature and relay this information to the computer. The computer then modifies the heating and air conditioning systems to adjust the temperature and humidity so that we occupants are comfortable and the organization is not wasting its money on unnecessarily heating or cooling the building. We are just beginning to see the development of these systems in our homes.

Electronic Funds Transfer

Finally, we come to a rather different application of the computer. Since the earliest days when people started to trade, money has had its own value as a commodity. The speed with which people pay for their goods has an effect on both cash flow and profitability so it is not surprising that attention has recently been paid to how we transfer money. We have all become used to paying by cheque for our purchases. A further move towards the cashless society has been the plastic credit card which has become a popular means of paying for goods. The next stage is the development of systems for Electronic Funds Transfer at Point-Of-Sale (EFTPOS). Here, a customer has a plastic card which has details of the customer's bank account encoded on its magnetic strip. The retailer has a device which is a magnetic card reader, a computer terminal and modem rolled into one (see Figure 16.1). The cost of the purchase is fed in, a check is made that funds are available to cover the cost of the transaction and, if so, the money transferred electronically that day from the customer's bank account to the retailer's. Good news for the retailer – no more bounced cheques and the money arrives straight away, just as it does with cash purchases. Mixed news for the customer – it should ensure a quicker service at the tills, no more fiddling around with cheque books and guarantee cards, but no free credit – you lose the money straight away!

Although EFTPOS has been slow to take off, there can be little doubt about the inevitability of it being a major method of payment

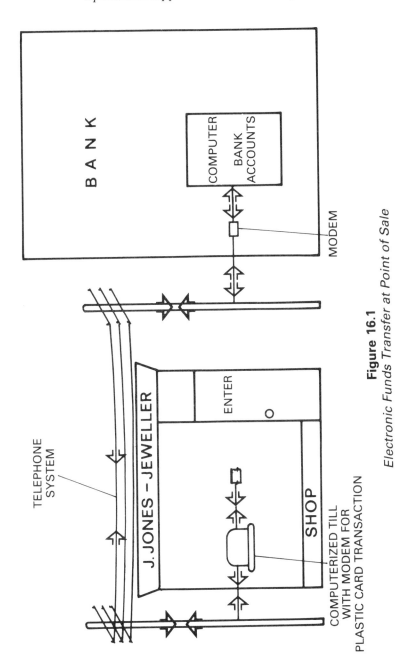

Figure 16.1
Electronic Funds Transfer at Point of Sale

within the next few years. For retailers and banks alike, the saving in paperwork and administration will be enormous. We suspect that our children will find chequebooks and possibly even cash transactions as anachronistic as we now find the horse and cart as a means of travel!

Conclusion

This has been only the briefest look at this fast expanding field. Developments are taking place at such a pace that it would be pointless to dwell on it further. We have tried to give you an insight into, and an understanding of, the enormous potential of the computer as an operational control device. Perhaps most of us have not yet reached the degree of confidence in such systems that we would willingly trust ourselves to an airliner which was completely controlled by computers and had no qualified pilot on board. On the other hand, perhaps that is just a state of mind. Our children or our children's children who have grown up with computers may regard them more benignly than we do. We are just beginning to see the development of applications in the home, for example, with environmental systems – perhaps robot helpers are not so far off. We could well be on the brink of a massive expansion and proliferation of the application of computers in every sector of our lives. Whether we view these as exciting or worrying, they are certainly on their way!

Glossary of Terms

ALTERNATIVE HYPOTHESIS: The alternative hypothesis covers all other plausible states of the population characteristic, other than the null hypothesis, for which the test is being carried out.

APPLICATION SYSTEMS GENERATOR: An application systems generator allows non-computer people to design their own systems and produce reports to their own specification.

ARRAY in ascending order: An array is where the data is set out in order of value, either increasing or decreasing in size. An array in ascending order puts the lowest value first and the highest value last.

BACKUP copies: Backup copies of computer data are copies on disk or tape that are stored remotely from the computer so that the data can be restored in the event of loss.

BAR CODE SCANNER: A bar code scanner reads bar codes off labels for direct inputting of the data contained in the codes to the computer.

BAR DIAGRAM: A bar diagram is a graphical representation of a frequency distribution where the horizontal axis shows non-numerical data, for example, sales representatives, factory, etc.

BINOMIAL experiment: A binomial experiment is one which possesses certain characteristics as set out on page 89.

BINOMIAL PROBABILITY DISTRIBUTION: This is the discrete probability distribution which describes the probabilities associated with the binomial experiment.

BOTTOM UP forecasting: Bottom up forecasting is a qualitative technique whereby managers at the lowest level are asked to give their view of the future for their area of responsibility. The forecasts are then put together to provide a forecast for the overall business. It is particularly used in short term forecasting.

CAUSAL APPROACH to forecasting: The causal approach to forecasting involves the use of historical data thought to explain or cause changes in the variable being forecast.

CENTRAL LIMIT THEOREM: The central limit theorem allows the application of the very useful properties of the normal distribution to the sampling distributions of the sample mean and proportion.

CENTRAL PROCESSOR UNIT (CPU): The central processor unit is the nerve centre of the computer which takes in instructions and data and performs appropriate calculations.

233

CHIP: The chip is a sliver of silicon on whose surface miniature electronic circuits have been etched, and which forms an integral part of all computers.

CLASSICAL METHOD OF ASSIGNING PROBABILITIES: This is a method of assigning probabilities to experimental outcomes which assumes that each outcome is equally likely.

CLICK: The sound made by a computer 'mouse' when operated to give instructions to a computer, now used in computer manuals as the instruction to press a button on the mouse.

CLUSTER SAMPLING: In cluster sampling, the population is divided into separate groups called clusters. A simple random sample of the clusters is then taken and the elements within the sampled clusters form the sample.

COEFFICIENT OF DETERMINATION: The coefficient of determination is a measure of how good a fit the regression line is to the data.

COMPATIBLE: Compatibility is the term used by computer people to identify when computer equipment and/or programs can work together.

COMPUTER AIDED DESIGN (CAD): CAD is the term used where computers are used to design products, buildings, components, etc.

COMPUTER AIDED MANUFACTURE (CAM): CAM is the term used where computers are used to assist in the control of the manufacturing process.

COMPUTER INTEGRATED MANUFACTURING (CIM): CIM is the term used where the entire industrial process from design to manufacture is controlled by computers.

COMPUTER NUMERICAL CONTROL (CNC): CNC is the term used to describe the process of quickly setting and resetting machines by computer, thereby making it more economic to manufacture small batches of the product.

COMPUTER PROCESS CONTROL (CPC): CPC is the term given to the control of processes by computers.

COMPUTER VIRUSES: A computer virus is the term used to describe a 'rogue' program which invades a computer, usually from a borrowed disk. The virus can corrupt or destroy data and programs.

CONFIDENCE LIMITS: Confidence limits provide a range within which a population characteristic, such as a mean, is expected to fall and with which is associated a probability or level of confidence.

CONTINGENCY TABLE: A contingency table is a table which sets out all the possible combinations and contingencies associated with an experiment or test. It is used in the test of independence.

CONTINUOUS RANDOM VARIABLE: A continuous random variable is a random variable that can take on an infinite number of values in an interval, for example, time, weight, distance.

CORPORATE DATABASE: A corporate database is a common store of the raw data possessed by an organization. It is available to all authorized personnel for analysis and use as required.

CORRELATION COEFFICIENT: The correlation coefficient measures the strength of the relationship between two variables.

CRITICAL PATH: The critical path in a network is the longest path and, therefore, one where any delay is critical to the completion of the project.

CUMULATIVE FREQUENCY DISTRIBUTION: In a cumulative frequency distribution the data is summarized in tabular form, showing the frequency or number of items with values less than or equal to a particular data point or upper limit of a class.

CYCLICAL ELEMENT: The cyclical element in a time series is a regular pattern of alternate sequences of observations above and below the trend line which lasts longer than a year.

DAISYWHEEL printer: A daisywheel printer converts output from the computer into readable text through the device of a hammer striking a spinning wheel to produce the characters on the paper.

DATA SET: The set of data of interest.

DATABASE MARKETING: In database marketing the computer selects names and addresses according to specified parameters from a database for subsequent merging with a standard letter or other promotional material held on a word processor.

DECISION THEORY: Decision theory or analysis is a technique used to arrive at an optimal (best) strategy when faced with a number of alternative strategies or decisions and an uncertain future situation.

DE-SEASONALIZING: De-seasonalizing is the term given to the technique of removing the seasonal element from a time series.

DECILES: Deciles are markers in an array which subdivide it into ten equal parts.

DECISION TREE: A decision tree is a graphical representation of a decision problem.

DEDICATED systems: Dedicated systems are designed, and used for one specific purpose, perhaps to serve a particular functional or departmental need. They are usually developed independently of other systems in the organization.

DELPHI APPROACH to forecasting: The Delphi approach to forecasting is a qualitative technique where a panel of experts give their view of the future and these views are refined until consensus is achieved.

DEPENDENT VARIABLE: The dependent variable is the variable being predicted by the relationship with the independent variables.

DESKTOP PUBLISHING (DTP): DTP is the term used to describe the use of a computer in the preparation of material for printing. It allows the text to be laid out in a wide variety of styles and forms and the incorporation of diagrams and photographs into the text.

DISCRETE PROBABILITY DISTRIBUTION: This is the probability distribution of a discrete random variable.

DISCRETE RANDOM VARIABLE: A discrete random variable is a random variable that takes on a finite number of values (say, 1 to 5) or an infinite sequence (say 1, 2, 3, etc). Examples are numbers of units sold, numbers of customers.

DISK DRIVE: A disk drive is a computer input device which reads instructions or data from a rotating disk.

DOCUMENT READER: A document reader reads alphanumeric characters from a document for inputting to the computer.

DOCUMENT SCANNER: A document scanner scans coded boxes of data from a document inputting the data directly into the computer.

DOT MATRIX printer: A dot matrix printer converts output from the computer into readable text, creating the characters through the impact of a matrix of pins through the printer ribbon.

ESTIMATES: The sample results provide estimates of what the parameters of interest might be if the whole population was surveyed.

EVENT: An event is a collection of outcomes or sample points.

EXCEPTION REPORT: A management report, generated to meet the information needs of some exceptional situation.

EXPECTED MONETARY VALUE: Expected monetary value is a decision criterion based on the sum of the weighted payoffs for each outcome of a decision, where the weights are the probability of that payoff or outcome occurring.

EXPERT SYSTEM: In an expert system, the rules and knowledge by which the human brain might arrive at decisions relating to a particular subject, are modelled in the computer thus allowing the computer to 'learn' from its experience.

FACSIMILE (OR FAX): A FAX machine is a device which can 'read' text, symbols and/or pictures from a document and convert them to electrical impulses which can be transmitted to other FAX machines for reproducing in documentary form.

FILE: A file is the term given to a discrete set of data which the computer operator has stored separately from all other sets.

FINITE population: A finite population is one where the size of the total population is limited i.e. not infinite.

FLOPPY disk: A floppy disk is a flexible magnetic disk containing either instructions or data for inputting to the computer and/or a medium for storing such instructions and/or data remotely from the computer.

FREQUENCY DISTRIBUTION: In a frequency distribution, the data is summarized in tabular form showing the frequency, i.e. the number of occurrences, of the data at each data or reference point or in each class.

FREQUENCY POLYGON: A frequency polygon is a graphical representation of a frequency distribution where the class intervals are shown on the horizontal axis and the frequencies are plotted as points against the mid-points of the classes.

GOODNESS OF FIT TEST: A goodness of fit test is a hypothesis test based on the Chi-squared distribution used to determine whether a hypothesized probability distribution provides a good fit for a population.

HACKER: A 'hacker' is a person who obtains unauthorized access to a computer, usually by bypassing the password protection devices.

HARD COPY: Hard copy is the term given to printed output from the computer.

HARD DISKS: A hard disk is a rigid magnetic disk containing instructions and/or data for the computer. Because the disk is 'hard' it is possible to compress a substantial amount of material on it.

HARDWARE: Computer hardware is the term given to the electronic/mechanical parts of the computer.

HISTOGRAM: A histogram is a graphical representation of a frequency distribution, where the class intervals are shown on the horizontal axis and the frequencies are plotted against the vertical axis in the form of rectangles.

INDEPENDENCE TEST: An independence test is a hypothesis test based on the Chi-squared distribution, used to test the independence of two variables.

INDEPENDENT VARIABLE: An independent variable is a variable which is being used to predict the dependent variable.

INDEX NUMBERS: Index numbers are used to measure changes in data over time by presenting the data as a proportion or percentage of some base value.

INKJET printer: The inkjet printer is a device for converting computer output to readable text by spraying dry powder onto the sheet where it is held by electrostatic charge and fixed by heat. It is relatively fast and very quiet in operation.

INPUT DEVICES: Input devices allow us to get instructions and data into the computer.

INTEGRATED PACKAGES: An integrated package is a set of computer instructions combined within the same program allowing data to be transferred easily, for example, between databases and spreadsheets, word processing and communication systems.

IRREGULAR ELEMENT: The irregular element in a time series is that element which cannot be explained by the trend, the cyclical and/or seasonal elements. It represents the random variability in the time series caused by unanticipated and non-recurring factors.

KEYBOARD: The keyboard is the most commonly used input device to the computer. Most computer keyboards closely resemble typewriter keyboards.

KILOBYTE: The kilobyte is a measure used to describe the capacity of computers and their storage disks.

LANGUAGE: The term 'language' is used to distinguish the different systems of programming computers.

LASER printer: A laser printer uses laser technology to convert output from the computer into readable text. Laser printers are very fast in operation.

LEAST SQUARES METHOD: The least squares method is a technique used to find the straight line which provides the best linear approximation for the relationship between two variables.

LIGHT PEN: A light pen can be used on a VDU to allow the operator to draw on the screen.

MAILMERGE: Mailmerge is the term used to describe the integration of standard letters with addresses from a database to produce personalized letters, for example, for a marketing mail shot.

MANAGEMENT INFORMATION: The right information in the right form and at the right time, so enabling the manager effectively and efficiently to do his/her job.

MATHEMATICAL MODELS: Mathematical modelling is the term used to describe the use of mathematical equations to model business or industrial situations.

MAXIMAX/MINIMIN: Maximax/minimin are decision criteria which seek to maximize the maximum payoff (maximax) or minimize the minimum payoff (minimin).

MAXIMIN/MINIMAX: Maximin/minimax are decision criteria which seek to maximize the minimum payoff (maximin) or minimize the maximum payoff (minimax).

MEAN (or AVERAGE): The arithmetic mean (or average) is the most commonly used measure of location for the middle of a data set and is obtained by adding together all the individual items of data and then dividing by the number of items in the data set.

MEAN SQUARED ERROR: The mean squared error is one measure of the accuracy of a forecasting model and is based on the average of the squared differences between the forecast values and the actual values of a time series.

MEASURES OF DISPERSION: Measures of dispersion tell us how variable or dispersed is the data in the set. Examples are range, variance and standard deviation.

MEASURES OF LOCATION: A measure of location is a way of defining particular points in an array of data. The most common are those relating to the middle of the array, the average or mean, the median and the mode. Others are percentiles, quartiles and deciles.

MEDIAN: The median is a measure of location which divides an array of data, so that half of the data items are smaller and half are greater in value than the median.

MENU: A menu is a list of options presented by a computer program on the VDU.

MODE: The mode is the item in a data set which occurs with the greatest frequency.

MODEM: A modem is a modulator/demodulator device used to connect computers together by telephone lines.

MONTE CARLO method: The Monte Carlo method is a commonly used technique for simulating the outcomes of operations we are trying to model.

MOUSE: The mouse is a hand operated computer device used to select, for example, from a menu displayed on the VDU screen.

MULTINOMIAL POPULATION: A multinomial population is a population where each member is assigned to one, and only one, of several classes or categories.

MULTIPLE REGRESSION: Multiple regression is the technique used in situations where two or more independent variables are used to predict the dependent variable.

NETWORK ANALYSIS: Network analysis is the term used to describe those techniques used for planning complex projects logically by analysing the component parts and laying them out in the form of a network diagram.

NETWORKING: Networking is a term used to describe the linking together of computers in order that, for example, they may have access to a common database.

NORMAL DISTRIBUTION: The normal distribution is a continuous probability distribution which is bell shaped and has the characteristics set out on pages 93–5.

NULL HYPOTHESIS: The null hypothesis is the tentative assumption made about the population characteristic to be tested.

OFF-LINE: Off-line is a term used to describe the operation of computer equipment which is not connected at that moment in time to the CPU. An example is data being prepared for input remotely and, therefore, not tying up the computer with the slowness of the data preparation equipment.

OGIVE: An ogive is a graph of the cumulative frequency distribution, or cumulative relative frequency distribution.

ONE-TAILED TEST: A one-tailed test is a type of hypothesis test where the alternative hypothesis is for a value either greater or smaller than that of the null hypothesis.

OPTICAL CHARACTER RECOGNITION (OCR): Optical characters are normal letters and figures that are altered slightly in shape so that when read by OCR equipment they produce unique signals which are recognizable by a computer.

OUTPUT DEVICES: Output devices are the means by which data and/or information can be obtained from the computer. One example of an output device is the printer.

PACKAGES: A computer package is a complete set of computer instructions which take the operator from input of data through calculations to output of results.

PAYOFF TABLE: A payoff table sets out the payoffs for the different decisions or strategies of a particular decision problem.

PERCENTILES: Percentiles are markers within an array which divide the data into 100 numerically equal parts. For example, the 17th percentile is the value such that 17% of the data items fall below it and 83% above. The median is the 50th percentile.

PERT: Programme Evaluation and Review Technique (PERT) is a system for planning and controlling complex projects through the use of network analysis.

PICTOGRAM: A pictogram uses the device of relevant pictures, for example £ signs representing money, as an eye catching way of presenting information. The size of the pictures represents the value of the item being depicted.

PIE CHART: A pie chart is the graphical representation of a frequency distribution in the form of a 'pie' or circle. Slices of the pie represent categories of data and are proportionate to the percentage of the whole pie that each category occupies.

PLOTTER: The plotter is a computer output device used to produce very accurate diagrams and graphs, often in colour.

POINT ESTIMATES: A point estimate is a single value estimate of a population characteristic such as a mean or a proportion.

POPULATION: In statistics, the population is defined as the collection of all items of interest for a particular purpose.

PREDICTION ERROR: Prediction error is the difference between the actual value and the predicted value.

PRINTER: The printer is one of the most common output devices from the computer, presenting the output in readable form.

PROBABILITY DENSITY FUNCTION: The probability density function is the means by which the probability of a continuous random variable assuming a specific value is calculated.

PROBABILITY DISTRIBUTION: A probability distribution for a random variable describes how the probabilities are distributed or spread over the various values that the random variable can assume.

PROBABILITY: Probability is a measure of uncertainty. It is a measure of the chance or likelihood that a particular event will occur.

PUNCHED CARDS: Punched cards are cards with coded holes cut into them which, when light is shone through the holes, allowed data or instructions to be recognized by the computer.

QUARTILES (UPPER/LOWER): The upper quartile is a marker in an array above which one quarter of the items fall, and below which fall three quarters. The lower quartile is a marker in an array below which fall one quarter of the items and above which fall three quarters.

RANDOM VARIABLE: A random variable is a numerical description that defines the outcome of an experiment or test.

RANDOM: See simple random sample.

RANGE: The range is a measure of dispersion and is the difference between the lowest and highest values in the data set.

RAW data: Raw data is data as originally recorded, in its original state – 'uncooked', i.e., not manipulated or tampered with in any way.

REGRESSION ANALYSIS: Regression analysis is a technique which enables us to describe the relationship between variables using a mathematical equation.

RELATIONSHIP DATABASES: Relationship databases are separate files in the database containing data on a particular subject or person. The files are linked in such a way that when data is changed in one of the files it is automatically changed in all of the files where it occurs.

RELATIVE FREQUENCY DISTRIBUTION: In a relative frequency distribution the data is summarized in tabular form showing the relative frequency – that is, the proportion of the total number of items at each data point or in each class of the data.

RELATIVE FREQUENCY METHOD: This is a method of assigning probabilities to experimental outcomes by conducting experiments or tests.

REQUEST REPORT: A request report is produced as a result of a specific request for information which is available but not usually included in a routine report.

ROUTINE REPORT: Routine reports form a regular part of a manager's information system. They are usually produced at pre-determined time intervals, contain the same sort of information and are presented in the same format on each occasion.

SAMPLE POINTS: Sample points are the individual outcomes of an experiment.

SAMPLE SPACE: A sample space is the set of all possible sample points, that is, outcomes of an experiment.

SAMPLE: A sample is a portion of the population selected to represent the whole.

SAMPLING DISTRIBUTIONS: Sampling distributions are the probability distributions of sample statistics.

SAMPLING ERROR: The sampling error is the magnitude of the difference between the estimate and the actual value of the population statistic of interest.

SAMPLING FRAME: A sampling frame is a list of the whole population being surveyed.

SCATTER DIAGRAM: A scatter diagram is a graph with the independent variable on the horizontal axis and the dependent variable on the vertical axis and showing a plot of the data points.

SCREENS: A 'screen' is a device for working on data held in the computer. It consists only of a keyboard and a VDU and cannot operate independently of the main computer.

SEASONAL ELEMENT: The seasonal element in a time series is a regular pattern of alternate sequences of observations above and below the trend line which lasts for a year or less.

SECTOR: A sector is a part of a track on a computer disk which is of the precise dimension to receive appropriate blocks of electrical impulses representing computer characters.

SHELL: The shell is the term used to describe the mechanisms which incorporate the different elements of an integrated computer package.

SIGNIFICANCE LEVEL: The significance level is the maximum probability of a Type 1 error that the user will accept when carrying out a hypothesis test. It is a measure of confidence in the result.

SIMPLE LINEAR REGRESSION: Simple linear regression is the technique used in situations where there are only two variables, one independent and one dependent, and the relationship between them can be described as a straight line.

SIMPLE RANDOM SAMPLE: A simple random sample selected from a population is a sample selected in such a way that every sample of that size has the same probability of being selected.

SIMULATION: Simulation is a technique of representing a system or process by a statistical model in order to produce a realistic set of outcomes from the model in different circumstances.

SKEWED: Data is said to be skewed when the distribution of the data is not symmetrical about the mean.

SLAVE STATIONS: A slave station is a device for interacting with the computer. Slave stations cannot operate independently of the main computer and usually consist of a keyboard and a VDU.

SMART CARD: A smart card can be used with a computer input device to tell the computer details held on the card such as credit information or security clearance.

SMOOTHING METHODS: Smoothing methods are used to smooth out the irregular element of time series and are appropriate to use where there are no significant trends, cyclical or seasonal patterns.

SOFTWARE: Computer software is the term given to the operating systems and the computer programs that make computers do what is asked of them.

SPECIAL REPORT: A special report usually arises out of some special situation and which requires information which is not readily available and may require an exercise in data capture.

SPREADSHEET: A spreadsheet is a matrix of rows and columns whose intersections, known as cells, may contain numbers or text. It allows rapid calculation of the data, following strict formulae which relate the cells in a specified way.

STANDARD DEVIATION: Standard deviation is a measure of how dispersed the data is about the mean. It is the square root of the variance.

STANDARD NORMAL DISTRIBUTION: The standard normal distribution is a normal distribution with the particular features of a mean of 0 and a standard deviation of 1.

STATISTICAL INFERENCE: Statistical inference is the process of making estimates or drawing conclusions about a population from a sample.

STRATIFIED RANDOM SAMPLING: In stratified random sampling the population is divided into strata and a random sample is chosen from each strata.

SUBJECTIVE METHOD: This is a method of assigning probabilities to experimental outcomes using one's judgement.

SUNRISE INDUSTRY: An industry which is developing and growing.

SUNSET INDUSTRY: An industry which is contracting and in decline.

SWIPE CARD: The swipe card is 'wiped' through a sensing device at a till and the amount registered on the till is automatically deducted from the purchaser's account.

SYSTEMATIC SAMPLING: Systematic sampling is a method of taking a sample from a large population whereby the first sample member is selected randomly and the remainder selected at regular intervals until the sample size is achieved.

TERMINALS: Terminals are input/output devices connected to a computer allowing several operators to access the CPU at the same time. The terminals are described as 'intelligent' if they are capable of carrying out data processing independently of the main computer.

TEXT PROCESSING: Text processing is the creation and manipulation of text using a computer or word processor.

TIME SERIES method of forecasting: The time series method of forecasting uses a sequence of values of a variable at successive points or periods of time to forecast what will happen to that variable in the future.

TOP DOWN forecasting: Top down forecasting is a qualitative technique whereby top management sets out its view of the future. The forecasts are then broken down to lower level forecasts. It is particularly used in short term forecasting.

TREE DIAGRAM: A diagrammatic representation showing the sample points or outcomes of a series of experiments.

TREND: The trend in a set of time series data is the long term movement or shift in the values observed over the time period in question.

TURN-KEY: A turn-key system is one which allows its operator to use it simply, as it were, by turning a key – no other knowledge or expertise is required.

TWO-TAILED TEST: The two-tailed test is a type of hypothesis test where the values of the alternative hypothesis are both greater than and smaller than that of the null hypothesis.

TYPE 1 ERROR: A Type 1 error occurs when the null hypothesis is rejected even when it is true.

TYPE 2 ERROR: A Type 2 error occurs when the null hypothesis is accepted even when it is false.

UNIFORM DISTRIBUTION: A uniform distribution is a continuous probability distribution where the probability that the random variable will assume a value in any interval of equal length is the same for each interval within the range of values for which the distribution is defined.

USER FRIENDLY: User friendly is the term given to computer programs that can be used by the non-expert computer user. There are usually clear instructions printed on the VDU screen to take the operator through each stage in the process.

VARIANCE: Variance is a measure of how dispersed the data is about the mean. It is the square of the standard deviation.

VISUAL DISPLAY UNIT (VDU): The VDU is a principal output device from most computers where the output is presented on a TV-like screen.

WINDOWS: Windows are subdivisions of the VDU screen which allow data to be displayed from different files held in the computer.

WORD PROCESSING: Word processing is the term given to the input, storage, manipulation, and printing out as hard copy of text by a computer or dedicated word processor.

WORK STATIONS: Work station is the term used to describe those devices at which operators can input data and/or instructions to the computer and receive responses back.

Index

245